T0146830

The Long Blue Walk

My Journey as a Philly Cop

Norman A. Carter Jr.

THE LONG BLUE WALK
MY JOURNEY AS A PHILLY COP

iUniverse books may be ordered through booksellers or by contacting:

iUniverse
1663 Liberty Drive
Bloomington, IN 47403
www.iuniverse.com
1-800-Authors (1-800-288-4677)

Because of the dynamic nature of the Internet, any web addresses or links contained in this book may have changed since publication and may no longer be valid. The views expressed in this work are solely those of the author and do not necessarily reflect the views of the publisher, and the publisher hereby disclaims any responsibility for them.

Any people depicted in stock imagery provided by Thinkstock are models, and such images are being used for illustrative purposes only. Certain stock imagery © Thinkstock.

ISBN: 978-1-5320-0146-8 (sc)
ISBN: 978-1-5320-0147-5 (e)

Library of Congress Control Number: 2016911922

Print information available on the last page.

iUniverse rev. date: 07/30/2016

Dedicated to my children Monique, Norman, Yvette, and Dana

Contents

Introduction

I am a retired Philadelphia Police Officer. I am proud of the twenty-five years I served the citizens of Philadelphia, Pennsylvania. My desire to become a Police Officer was not solely based on securing gainful employment to provide financial stability for my family. Three years before I became a Police Officer, while sitting in a barracks at Fort Carson, Colorado, I made that decision. During the early and middle 1960's, Police Officers were widely portrayed as the government's tool of oppression. The country was in the midst of change. I felt that one of the best ways I could be a part of that change was to become a member of the law enforcement arm in my city.

While a Police Officer in Philadelphia I had an opportunity to work among many honorable and heroic men and women. They were the unsung heroes who worked to provide the citizens in Philadelphia a healthy environment in which to live. In so doing, they were doing their best to provide an environment where citizens felt free and safe. Some of these men and women died serving their city. Some suffered severe physical and mental traumas that would affect them throughout their lives. Just as with war veterans, their sacrifices were soon forgotten by the public.

What stands out with the public are not the names but the deeds of those who soiled the reputation of the noble profession of Police Officer. Of them, I will speak a great deal. While, I knew many Police Officers who did their job honorably, I worked with some who were in league with criminals. It is dangerous to talk publicly about criminalized Police Officers. It is, also, not popular. Many look at such exposure as counterproductive. Those same people will tell you that the public should focus on the "good cops" who do a great job in their community. I agree with honoring and rewarding those "good cops". But the public myopia of not looking a bit further to seek and to root out "bad cops" serves to undermine the efforts of honest and committed police professionals.

For years, I tried to expose poor police practices and criminalized Police Officers. I was met with administrative lethargy, systemic retaliation, and character assassination. This chronicle is my true account of how the "blue wall of silence" was maintained at every leadership level within the Philadelphia Police Department. I will attempt to show how this systemic inertia negatively impacted every citizen of Philadelphia.

Years after my police career ended, I found those same practices repeated in such cities as Houston, Texas and Atlanta, Georgia. This latter revelation I learned during my participation in a Dateline NBC expose' entitled "Playing the Numbers" (1-13-99 catalog #NDL990113).

I believe it is imperative for every Police Officer and their families to read this chronicle which details the internal pressures faced by new and veteran officers. My hope is that the Police Officers of Philadelphia and your community are not plagued by such dangerous corporate dishonesty and ineptitude. In a recent sermon, Reverend Charles L. Brown of the Cornerstone Church of Snellville preached a sermon based on 2nd Chronicles, 20th Chapter, and 17th verse. It reads, "The battle is not for you to fight; take your position, stand still, and see the victory of the Lord on your behalf, O Judah and Jerusalem. Do not fear or be dismayed; tomorrow go out against them, and the Lord will be with you." I was outnumbered, but I held my ground and never compromised my integrity. My city benefited. This was my journey. This was my long blue walk.

Childhood Memories

My elementary school teachers frequently quoted an old saying which said, "As the twig is bent, so grows the tree." I can truly say that my childhood experiences molded me and set me on a path that influenced my career as a Police Officer. When I was about 6 years old, my father told me to never follow the crowd when I knew they were doing wrong. About the same time, he and my mother told me that all people, regardless of race or color were equal. All should be treated fairly. Fortunately, those values stayed with me throughout the curve balls I encountered growing up in my poverty stricken neighborhood in North Central Philadelphia, Pennsylvania.

Becoming a Police Officer was not a childhood ambition of mine. In elementary school, Officer Burke visited us every year. He would give us safety instructions about how to cross streets properly, obeying litter laws (new at that time), and trusting Police Officers especially if you became lost. I wished all Police Officers could have been as jovial and personable as Officer Burke. Such was not the case.

One afternoon, a disturbance occurred in a house on my street. Police Officers from the 23rd Police District responded. One member of the family became involved in a struggle with the Police Officers. He tried to run from them, but he was caught after a short chase. The Police Officers caught him about twenty-five yards away from where a crowd of us were standing. Several Officers pummeled him. They were beating him around the head and body with batons and blackjacks. It was a horrific scene. In shock we watched as this unconscious man was put on a stretcher and placed inside a police van (we called it the "paddy wagon"). This was the type of scene that makes one fear, not respect Police Officers. Of course, community relations was not ever the focus of these Officers. This incident left me with a very bad impression about Police Officers. It, also, made me aware of what would happen to me or anyone else if we ever fought Police Officers. The rampant rumor was that if you were arrested, Police Officers would interrogate you by beating you across the bottom of your feet with a rubber hose. After I became a Police Officer, this type of activity was known as "street justice" or "making clubs trump."

These memories stayed with me throughout my police career.

Military Career

On July 31, 1963, I left North Philly and childhood behind me. I joined the United States Army. There must have been about fifty to sixty young men inducted into the United States Army during that morning at 401 North Broad Street in Philadelphia. Surprisingly, I knew many of the inductees. Incidentally, several of the inductees were from my high school graduating class. At that time, I could not imagine that several years later Thomas A. Edison High School, my high school, would have a bitter sweet notoriety in America. More students from my high school were killed in the Vietnam War than from any other high school in America. Some of the young men I stood with on that day would never complete their enlistment. They would die serving their country. I pray that God gave them the glory they never knew in their young lives. Others would return emotionally and physically damaged.

I learned many life lessons while in the Army. I grew emotionally and physically. During my enlistment, I was fortunate enough to attend and to graduate from the United States Military Academy Preparatory School (West Point Prep). That school opened educational avenues that I had not traveled while attending Philadelphia's Public Schools. Unfortunately, I did not finish high enough in my class to obtain an appointment to the United States Military Academy at West Point, New York. While there I learned lessons about leadership and integrity that I have practiced throughout my life.

After leaving the Prep School, I ended my military career as a Medical Specialist/Personnel Specialist at Fort Knox, Kentucky. I achieved the rank of Specialist 5th Class and left the military late in July of 1966.

Transitioning to Civilian Life

When I left the military, I returned home to Philadelphia. My wife (I married her in the summer of 1965 after graduating from Prep School), was a few weeks shy of delivering our first child. Before I returned home, she secured an apartment for us at the Schuylkill (pronounced "school kill") Falls Housing Projects in the East Falls section of the city. Long before my discharge from the military, I had decided that I wanted to become a Police Officer. The late 1950's and early 1960's were a time when Black Americans began to use civil disobedience to achieve equal treatment in the areas of education, access to public facilities, housing, employment, and law enforcement. While I observed many attempting to foster changes from outside of "the system", I surmised that it was equally as important to work for change while being a part of "the system." I thought that being a part of the law enforcement area of government would give me an opportunity to be a part of a progressive change towards equal treatment for all citizens regardless of their race, religion, or country of origin. I was not being quixotic. America was changing. I wanted to be an active part of that change. I wanted to be a Peace Officer.

After my daughter, Monique, was born and after we had gone through the first few weeks of her growth, I thought it would be a good time to begin my quest to join the Philadelphia Police Department. My wife was not thrilled with my career choice. She feared that because I was outspoken on such topics as civil rights and fair treatment, that I would be at odds with the perceived practices of the Philadelphia Police Department.

Rather that run into the first serious argument of our young married life, I looked for other employment. I moved through several jobs. My first job was that as an agent for a Loan Company. That job did not appeal to me. Next, I worked for several months as a grocery clerk for Pantry Pride. I stopped working there because the company changed my job location every month. I began working in the Frankford section of the city. After a month, I was transferred to the Somerton section of the city. After another month, I was transferred to the Southeastern section of South Philadelphia. This was obviously an unstable company. I resigned from this company and took the test for the Philadelphia Police Department. I did not tell anyone that I had taken this examination. I was immediately told that I had passed the examination. The only thing holding me back was that I had not obtained a Pennsylvania Driver's License when I was discharged from the Army. In December of 1966, I obtained my Pennsylvania Driver's License.

At the beginning of March 1967, I received a letter from the Police Department. It informed me that I had been accepted for admission to the Police Academy. I was slated to begin training with Recruitment Class 183 on March 20, 1967. I was overjoyed. My wife was moderately happy, although she still harbored some misgivings about the Police Department. At that time, I was working for a Dental Laboratory making dental prosthetics. I notified the owners of the Dental Laboratory of my acceptance at the Academy and gave them my two week notice. They laughed at me. I was 5'10" tall and weighed about 149 pounds. I was too small, they thought. One co-worker told me the Police Department wanted "tough guys" and I was a long way from being a tough guy. This was almost embarrassing.

Late one afternoon, as I was waiting for the Route 61 bus at Broad Street and Ridge Ave., I met a childhood neighbor. He was several years older than I and lived across the street from me on Harlan St. when I was a child. He looked at me with disgust after I told him that I would be joining the Police Department. "Norman, be a fireman. Be a trash man. Be anything but a cop." The words seared my soul. I was not getting a vote of confidence from any friends or co-workers. My family showed lukewarm satisfaction. Police Officers were known as people who could not be trusted. They were looked upon as being corrupt and brutal. That was the prevailing feeling of most people in my neighborhood. Fortunately, I knew in my heart that this was the right decision for me. I had thought about it while I was in the Army and now I was about to achieve my ambition. I was about to become a Philadelphia Police Officer.

The Police Academy

Just as I feel now, I felt then. A career as a Police Officer sets one in an occupation that is dedicated to honorably enforcing those laws and policies documented in the United States Constitution and the laws and policies of one's local government. There is no room for collusion with criminals or for self-serving interpretations of the previously mentioned laws and policies. This is a career that demands the highest levels of integrity and dedication. Without those qualities one's community is jeopardized by lackadaisical and capricious law enforcement. This is dangerous. Once a Police Officer works in league with criminals and scoundrels he/she becomes a criminal and a scoundrel. One cannot straddle that fence called integrity. One dirty foot pollutes the entire body.

For our first day, we were told to report wearing a white shirt, black tie, black pants, and black leather shoes. I had to travel there by public transportation. This resulted in a two-hour ride to the Police Academy at State Road and Ashburner Street. I had to walk the last three blocks as the bus stopped at Frankford Avenue and Ashburner Street. The latter location happened to be a short distance from the Pantry Pride store I had worked a few months before. I was prepared to meet all strangers. I found one person, David, whom I knew from high school. We were not friends. We just recognized each other. I would later learn that most of the class had prior military service.

There were about four hundred recruits looking like a small flock of penguins on a chilly March morning. About 8:30am, a loud Police Sergeant called us to assemble. We were placed into four groups, similar to a military four platoon formation by alphabetical order. This determined our seating placement in the Police Academy's auditorium. This Sergeant, would constantly refer to us as looking like "F-Troop" (referring to a television comedy series about a group of Army Calvary misfits in the late 19th century). On bad days, he would call us "shit heads". On good days, he would call us by the same name, but add "that's a term of endearment, gentlemen." Still, this was all milder than the gruff treatment I received at the beginning of my enlistment in the Army. This was the beginning of our socialization into the Police Department.

On the first day, we were sworn in and given our badges. Identification cards would come later that week. In the outdoor area on Academy grounds were a host of vendors ready to sell everything from food to police gear. They made a lot of money from us. Many recruits could barely wait to purchase gun holsters and handcuff cases, even though it would be about two weeks before we would need either item. By the third day, I was able to car pool with a group of recruits from the Manayunk area of the city. A month later, I purchased a car.

Training at the Academy seemed intense, but it was nothing I could not handle. The physical training we went through was mild in comparison to what I experienced in the Army less than a year before. I had to accustom myself to some of the language. Criminals were often called "critters". Some civilians were either "assholes" or "jerk offs". You learned to trust no one except another Police Officer. This began the bonding that solidified Police Officers into a group that isolates itself from the general public and supposedly insulates itself from outside influences. I would later learn that this type of isolation/insulation more often worked to the detriment of the public and the Police Department.

Out of all the training we received, the only portion I had mixed feelings about was our Organized Crime seminars. The Instructor was from an investigative division that frequently was the subject of questionable law enforcement practices. This group of Vice Investigators were legendary in Philadelphia. News coverage of his squad showed they were constantly under investigation for corruption. "Vice" crimes are often referred to as "victimless crimes". These are crimes such as setting up and maintaining an illegal lottery; prostitution; selling, manufacturing, or using illegal narcotics; and the selling alcoholic beverages without a license. Many Police Officers in this squad resigned from the department in order to save their pensions. If one was arrested while a Police Officer, one would most often lose his pension. This was devastating to Officers with more than ten years of service and who had not reached the retirement age of 55 years old. My recruit class was the first to be hired under a new pension plan which allowed one to retire at 45 years old. Okay, I was in a quandary as to why this person was selected to give us instruction on Organized Crime. After all, his character and the character of his unit seemed in question. This was my first lesson in how the Police Department sometimes took care of those who were loyal i.e., kept their mouths shut when they were subjects of an investigation that could prove to be embarrassing to their superiors.

The Instructor would discuss his career and his experiences with such crime legends as Lillian Reis, Al Capone, Willie "The Actor" Sutton, and Angelo Bruno. Lumped into these discussions were arrests of such entertainment celebrities as Lenny Bruce (for using profanity in his comedy act); Billie Holiday and Ray Charles for possession of illegal narcotics. We discussed the Philadelphia Mafia and its influence in illegal lotteries, off track horse race betting, illegal liquor sales, illegal narcotics sales, and prostitution.

I grew up seeing people in my predominantly Afro-American neighborhood who made a living "running numbers" (taking illegal lottery bets and paying off the winners). These were the minions of the illegal lottery business. There was always more emphasis on arresting these people rather than the organizers who reaped the greater financial benefits of this criminal enterprise. I had a lot to learn about how the Police Department selectively enforced some laws.

While at the Academy, I received one of my first lessons in how the stringent application and background investigation process was not a guarantee that some dishonest people would not be hired. We were in our sixth week at the Academy. All of us had our guns, badges, and handcuffs. We were wearing uniforms. We had but two weeks to go before graduating from the Academy. About 1:30pm, two recruits were called out of class. This was unusual but it had happened before when clarification was required for some administrative oversight. About ten minutes later, another recruit was called out of class. By 3:30pm, our class was notified about what had transpired. Two recruits were seen stealing gun holsters and other items from one of the vendors on our Academy grounds. These vendors operated their businesses out of small trucks. The recruits were

8

seen placing the items in a private vehicle. The investigation showed that the vehicle's owner had no idea that the stolen items were placed in his vehicle. The other two recruits normally rode to work in his vehicle. The two recruits who stole the items were arrested and dismissed from the Police Department. Everyone was shocked. This was the first and only such incident that occurred in our class. The recruit who owned the car went on to have a very good career. He retired as a Police Lieutenant. He was a part of a small circle of Police Officers who interacted with my family throughout my Police career.

Graduation day from the Police Academy reminded me of my graduation from the U.S. Military Academy Preparatory School in 1965. We had a graduation class of over three hundred Police Officers. Many of the graduating Officers were from counties outside of Philadelphia. Just as at the graduation in 1965, I had no family there. Everyone graduating was excited about the prospect of being assigned to a Police District. Hopefully, the assignment would be close to home. Police Officers were prohibited from working in the Police District where they resided. This was to prevent conflicts of interests and possible retaliatory activities directed at the Officer or his family. I thought this was a very good policy. Almost every "rookie" Officer was assigned to a Police District. A significant number were assigned to a division we had never heard of called "Task Force". Two of us, Jimmy R. and I, were assigned to another mysterious outfit called "The Vandalism Squad". It was a small squad in the Task Force Unit. Jimmy R. and I reported to Task Force Headquarters at 7:00am on Monday to meet with a Captain, a Lieutenant and a Sergeant for assignment instructions.

Task Force

The "Task Force" unit was a new and unique experiment in the Police Department. The unit was composed almost completely of newly hired Police Officers. The majority were fresh out of the Academy. The unit's veterans had less than two years on the Police Force. Officers in this unit received daily assignments throughout the city. On the evening shift, (6pm – 2am on weekdays and 7pm – 3am on Friday and Saturday nights) Task Force Officers were a crime suppression force. Assignments were based on Police District Commanders' targeted high crime activity areas. This allowed regular District Officers to concentrate on community calls for police service. On the day shifts, teams of Task Force Officers were assigned to high schools throughout the city. The focus for this shift was to ensure that students were able to arrive at, remain in, and leave schools safely. All of those appeared to be exciting assignments.

Jimmy R.'s and my assignment was the Vandalism Squad. The Vandalism Squad was a sub-division of the Task Force Unit. This squad was a pilot project that resulted from citizens' complaints about abandoned properties that were vandalized by scavengers who stole piping, toilets and electrical fixtures from those properties. We would work in two-man teams and our focus would be restricted to the South Philadelphia Division. The South Police Division was comprised of four Police Districts. They were the 1st, 3rd, 4th, and 17th Police Districts. The South Police Division covered a large area bordered by South Street on the north end, the Delaware River on the east end, the Navy Yard on the south end, and the Schuylkill River on the west end. Our job was to patrol those areas and focus on identifying and reporting vacant properties that were not secured. We would investigate those unsecured properties for damage and vandalism.

At the end of each day we would turn in a Police Incident Report (75-48) for each property. In addition, we were to investigate scavengers to insure they had a "Scavengers' License". Back in my North Philly neighborhood, we called them Junk Men. Supposedly, we were to issue a summons' to anyone who was transporting discarded metal, paper, or rags and who did not have a Scavengers' License. Our work hours would be either 6am – 2pm or 7am – 3pm, Monday to Friday. We were off every weekend. For some this would be a dream job. For a 22 year old rookie cop with a ton of energy, it was a nightmare.

Almost every day, I was partnered with Officer Jack Marino (not his real name). He was basically a nice guy. He wasn't cocky, just convinced. He drove the police car 90% of the time. My job was to listen and to observe. Here are the highlights/lowlights of my tenure in the Vandalism Squad.

a. Every morning, we assembled at our headquarters in the South Detective Division at 24th and Wolf Streets. On my first two days, Jack showed me around the southern portion of the South Division. We often drove by his mother's home. I would sit in the car. He would go into the house. One day, an idiot wearing a "Nazi Soldier's" helmet drove past us on a loud Harley Davidson motorcycle. The vehicle did not have a muffler and sped through his mother's narrow street as if a race was occurring. I was seated in the passenger seat of the red Police Car. Jack came outside. I was anxious to write my first moving violation. Jack calmed me down. He told me that we could not touch this guy. He was affiliated with the South Philadelphia Mafia. He was untouchable. A crook? Untouchable? Was the tail wagging the dog?

b. During our first week together, Jack took me to a delicatessen on Snyder Ave. While inside, he pointed to a property that was across the street. There were illegally parked cars on each side of this corner property. He told me to never take any police action, including writing tickets around this property. It was untouchable. It was the headquarters of Angelo Bruno. Angelo Bruno was the head of the Philadelphia Mafia. A crook? Untouchable? Was the tail wagging the dog?

c.   I was instructed never to respond to any radio calls that would require us to "get involved." That meant that he did not want us making any arrests. That would require one or both of us to appear in court. To him, appearing in court was an imposition. I thought it was our responsibility.

d.   Most of the work that we did on a normal day took about two hours. The idea was to generate enough paperwork to keep the "bosses happy". We were never to do too much because more would be expected. We had to keep a low profile. We did a lot of hanging around Pat's Steaks. Jack was friendly with the day manager.

e.   I quickly surmised that Jack did not like patrolling in the districts west of Broad Street. These had the most activity and one was more likely to get involved in confronting criminal activity.

f.   On the few days that Jack was off, I would respond to every emergency call. I was anxious to see what "real Police Officers" did. I wanted to look for and catch burglars, robbers, and thieves. That was why I joined the Police Force. I drove over the entire South Division. I turned in my required work and I took advantage of every opportunity to observe and to learn. I looked forward to the few days that I worked alone.

In early September, Jimmy R.'s and my assignment changed. We were reassigned from the Vandalism Squad to the actual Task Force Unit. I was relieved. I was going to be doing police work, at last. On the evening shift everyone worked with a partner. We were assigned to high crime areas. There was an emphasis on making quality vehicle and pedestrian investigations, enforcing curfew violations, and making arrests for "Part One" offenses. These offenses, as designated by the Federal Bureau of Investigation's Uniform Crime Reports were: murder, aggravated assault, robbery (armed and unarmed), arson, forcible rape, burglary, vehicle theft, and larceny-theft. The unit was full of energetic rookies who charged out each day looking for criminals. This was a total departure from my time on the vandalism detail. Most of the Officers in this unit came to work with polished uniforms and the best of equipment. These Officers purchased webbed leather gear rather than use the standard leather gear we had been issued. These Officers polished their leather coats as well as spit-shined their shoes. We competed with the more well-known Highway Patrol Division which was composed of veteran Officers who were normally assigned to high crime areas. They were the "shock troops" of the Police Department. They had a reputation for making a large number of Part One arrests and for having a "no nonsense approach" when dealing with the public. They were not public relations icons. They were feared. Our unit was often disparagingly referred to as "Junior Highway". Every day, I looked forward to coming to work. Everyday presented a new challenge.

In early October 1967, some of the Officers with whom I attended the Police Academy, invited me to a small house party at the North Philadelphia home of one of the Officers. I had not seen most of them since I left the Academy. All of them were assigned to Police Districts. All of us brought our wives or a date to the party. At the party, there was extensive talk about our experiences on the Police Department. I had the least to offer in the conversations. I had not been doing a lot of "real" police work. I was highly intrigued with the conversations. These African-American Police Officers all worked in pre-dominantly African-American neighborhoods. There seemed to be a severe lack of compassion or concern for the people who lived in those communities. They bragged about the number of parking tickets and moving violation summonses they wrote. Some said that if they wrote a significant number of tickets during a month that their Sergeant would grant them "Slide Time". This "Slide Time" meant being allowed to leave work for several hours or an entire day but be carried as working. "Slide Time" was a reward for making the Platoon Sergeant, Squad Commander, and District Commander look good for having shown a "high level" of police activity. It was a numbers game. The more tickets you wrote, the more valuable you were to your supervisors.

Many of the moving violations they bragged about were questionable. I remember interjecting at some point with a question. I stated that some people certainly deserved to receive traffic tickets, but I was not comfortable with writing tickets just to get a few hours off. I asked if they realized that they were issuing tickets to people who were depending on us to make their lives better and safer. Why were we acting in the same manner as the Officers our communities had learned to distrust? I asked if they realized that they were working among poor people and that whenever these people were issued a traffic summons, they were in jeopardy of having to pay higher insurance rates. Just to achieve favor with their Sergeants, they were negatively impacting the economic stability of many families. Sometimes people who committed serious violations deserved to be issued a summons. Sometimes people would make honest mistakes. Why penalize them for that? I was told that since I did not work in a district, I had no idea of how the Police Department worked. They agreed that I needed to work in a district in order to understand their position. Slightly more than a month later, my Sergeant told me that I was reassigned from the Task Force Unit to the 14th Police District. The reality of being a professional Police Officer was about to begin.

[While at the Police Academy, I was able to purchase a 1962 Chevrolet Impala. The car was a perpetual headache, but it supplied needed transportation. I bought it shortly after someone told me that since I was a Police Officer, everyone would give me credit. I had mixed feelings about credit. My goal was to purchase everything with cash. When you have a family, goals change. After purchasing the car, we looked for a new home. We had to move out of the housing project because of my income. One of the first places we selected came from an ad in the Sunday Philadelphia Inquirer. It is important to remember, that I am an idealist. Part of the Separation Orientation from the Army was to inform us about the equal job opportunity and equal housing laws that recently had been enacted.

We anxiously called the Real Estate Agent. His office was located in the far Northeast section of the city. We drove about twenty miles to the office. On our arrival the friendly agent told us about this lovely house in a sub-division called Morrell Park. This was 1967. We followed him as he drove to the house. Once we arrived in the sub-division, we parked about 50 yards from the house. He alit from his car first and walked back to us. He told us that he could not reach the home owner by phone. He needed to speak to her to obtain permission for us to walk through the house. We understood. As he walked away, he softly stated, "Just sit in your car and relax. I will be back to get you." It was a hot summer day. Our car was not equipped with air conditioning. As he approached the home we saw a woman, sitting in a chair on the lawn next to the house. The agent was in the house for a long period of time. Both my wife and I wanted to stretch our legs. We got out of the car and waited for the agent to return. On his return, he stated that the owner would not be able to show the house at that time. He would have to call the next day, Monday, to set up another appointment. We understood. We were still excited. Monday afternoon, the agent called me. In short he said, that he had a reason for telling us to stay in the car. He did not want neighbors to see us. Almost the entire sub-division was occupied by Caucasian families. We were African-American. Allegedly, the neighbor who was sitting outside near the home told the home owner that the agent wanted to show the home to an African-American family. The owner told the agent that she would not sell the home to anyone who was not Caucasian. I protested. "What about the equal housing laws?" He answered by explaining that the way home owners circumvented this law was by taking their home off the market and relisting it later.

Our friendly agent offered to sell us a home in the Yorktown sub-division. This was a predominantly African American sub-division that was located a very short distance from where I grew up. I remembered seeing that once dilapidated neighborhood being razed and rebuilt. I refused his offer. It was a weak attempt at appeasement. I did not want to be appeased. I wanted to be respected as a valued consumer. In spite of new legislation, a significant portion of America still looked at us as second class citizens. It did not matter that I had served three years in the Army. It did not matter that I was a Police Officer. In the minds of these Neanderthals, I was still a second-class citizen.]

14th Police District

It felt strange walking into a new district assignment. I did not know what to expect. Several of the Officers who attended the Academy with me were assigned to the 14th District. I was finally going to work among them and be able to engage in conversations about shared experiences. I would be chasing crooks, taking people to the hospital, driving around assigned sectors, and helping people. This was what I always wanted to do. In spite of the slight uneasiness that comes with walking into a new work environment, I was excited about everything. As a man with a family, the work hours would be a challenge. Police Officers worked swing shifts which meant that many nights I would be away from home. This presented a challenge for child care and overall family togetherness. Still, I felt it was a step up from Task Force.

I was assigned to "3 Squad". Each district had five squads. Four of the squads were Police Officers who alternated working the "8am – 4pm", "4pm – 12am", and the "12am – 8am (Last Out)" shifts. There was a "5 Squad". This squad was composed of Police Officers who worked directly under the District Commander or Captain. My first night, I found myself working the 12am – 8am or "Last Out" shift. All of my leather gear was highly polished. I wanted to make a good first impression. Each squad was broken into two sections. One section started fifteen minutes before the top of the hour and the other section started fifteen minutes after the hour. I was assigned to the "B" section which started fifteen minutes after the hour. Most of the Officers I knew were in the "A" section or early portion of the squad. I would later learn that the "A" section was responsible for all sectors east of Germantown Ave., and the "B" section was responsible for all sectors west of Germantown Ave.

Germantown Ave. was one of the longest streets in Philadelphia. The 14th Police District was one of the largest districts in Philadelphia. It was one of four Police Districts in the Northwest Police Division. There were towns and counties that were not as large as the 14th Police District. It contained several distinct neighborhoods: Germantown (with subsections of Brickyard, Pulaski Town, and Dog Town); East Mount Airy, West Mount Airy, and Chestnut Hill. The populace's economic extremes went from low income in Germantown to middle-income in East and West Mount Airy to high income in Chestnut Hill. Throughout the district there were historic buildings. Many structures were built during the Revolutionary War. The entire length of Germantown Avenue was cobblestoned. When the ground was wet, these cobblestones were very slippery to drive on. When the weather was dry, the constant pounding would throw your car out of alignment and vibrate your entire body. This moderately sized throughway had one parking lane on each side of the street. The middle portion of the street contained two sets of trolley tracks. These trolley tracks guided the northbound and southbound Route 23 Trolley. At 25.5 miles, this longest Philadelphia Trolley Route was infamous for its constant impedance of vehicular traffic throughout its route. In the 14th District, Germantown Ave. was the neighborhood and police sector boundary.

People on different sides of Germantown Ave. seldom interacted with one another. It is amazing how such artificial boundaries throughout Philadelphia defined neighborhoods, mores, and juvenile gang turf.

The 14th District Headquarters sat in the middle of a block lined with row houses. The eastern portion of the block housed Germantown's Town Hall. While secure, it had to be an awful street for residents. There was always the noise of police vehicle traffic especially during shift changes. This unit block of Haines Street was slightly larger than the narrow Harlan Street where I lived when I was a child. Between the Police Station and the Town Hall there was a relatively small parking lot. This parking lot was solely for Police Officers. There was seldom room for anyone else to park. At the time of my arrival to the 14th District, it was among the most modern looking Police Districts. It actually had a tiled floor and fresh paint. I had walked into many districts which had warped wooden floors and peeling paint.

On my first day at the 14th District, I reported in for the 12pm – 8am (Last Out) shift. With nervous anticipation, I looked forward to patrolling the streets of this new assignment. As at the Police Academy, all Officers stood in a two-rowed "platoon formation". Prior to receiving instructions for the day, the Platoon Sergeant and Squad Lieutenant inspected each Officer. This inspection consisted of insuring that each Officer was in proper uniform, had his weapon, and had other standard equipment. When I graduated from the Police Academy, my class was the first to be fully outfitted with leather jackets for winter wear. Most veteran Officers wore heavy dark blue wool coats called "reefers". After inspection, I was introduced to the squad.

Roll call consisted of the Sergeant notifying the squad about crime trends, outstanding events, and giving out assignments. As I stood during my first roll call in the 14th District, I was sweating in my new leather coat. I was visualizing myself driving around and learning this new area. I was familiar with some of the larger streets. As the Sergeant read down the list of assignments, he arrived at my name, "Carter, Foot Beat 2". Me!!?? On a Foot Beat in the middle of the night!!?? Didn't the Sergeant know I had six months experience driving a police vehicle? (That sounds funny, now.) I was dumbfounded. This foot beat was on Germantown Ave., between Chelten Ave. and Schoolhouse Ln. I was devastated. I could not wait to have a conversation with the Sergeant. He needed to know that I could handle a vehicle assignment. After Roll Call, I went to my assignment. My beat contained a large department store, "Allen's" at the corner of Germantown and Chelten Aves., Woolworth's Department Store, several banks, and small clothing stores.

Although disconsolate, I checked all business doors and made the proper entries on my patrol log on this chilly late autumn night. By 1:30am, I had walked up and down my beat about eight times. It was about this time that Pete, who attended the Academy with me, pulled up in his patrol car and asked me to get in. He wanted to give me a chance to get warm. I told him about my frustration at being on a foot beat. He told me to be patient. I had to prove myself to the Sergeant. Also, he told me that I could always get warm by going into the Doughnut Shop at Germantown and Chelten Avenues or go into Linton's Restaurant which was across the street from the Doughnut Shop. At that time, Police Officers were allowed a twenty-minute lunch break and a ten minute "personal" break.

I was a bit nervous about going into the Doughnut Shop, but the overnight clerk, whom I will call "Mary" was very friendly. She immediately offered me coffee. I was not a coffee drinker, so I declined. She insisted as she thought I was just shy. I gave in and took a cup of coffee. There was no charge. I was embarrassed by that. I tried to pay for it, but she would not accept money. I found out later that having Police Officers stop in frequently, was the best security one could have during the overnight shift. Police Officers were always in either Linton's or the Doughnut Shop. I did not spend too much time in the Doughnut Shop (its actual name). I did not want to make a bad impression with my superiors. I did not want to have any burglaries on my beat. That was always important to me throughout my career. By my third day, I was "recorder" in a patrol car. The "recorder" assists the driver by maintaining the patrol log and answering the radio. For new Officers, it was an opportunity to learn the district and forge a relationship with other Officers. It was mostly a time for the veterans in your squad to find out if you could be trusted. No one wanted a "fink" in their squad. That was the greatest fear. For me, that seemed stupid. You come to work. You do your job. You go home. How naïve was I?

This first night as a recorder, I was partnered with a veteran Officer. He must have had about fifteen years on the job. The first thing the veteran told me was not to answer the radio. He took over that responsibility while driving. So much for partnership. The idea of not having a "rookie" Officer answer the radio was that most veteran Officers wanted to keep a very low profile. Some were selective about calls they answered, even if those calls were on their sector of responsibility. This was frustrating. The other instruction, I was given was to write my log in pencil not pen. I hated writing in pencil. The reason behind writing in pencil was that there were times you might have to change a notation on your patrol log. Imagine that you entered a security check on your log and it was later found that the property was burglarized. It was better not to have checked the property rather than to have checked it and missed discovering an opening in the property. The "Integrity" portion of the Police Motto ("Honor, Integrity, and Service") was slowly going out the window. Still, I was a voiceless rookie. I followed instructions.

(My stubbornness in not falling into the "street rule" of writing in pencil paid off for me three years into my career in the 14ᵗʰ Police District. One summer Saturday night, while working the "Last Out" shift, I received a radio call for a disturbance at a residence on West Hansberry Street. Emergency Patrol Wagon 1402 accompanied me on this assignment. After we completed the assignment, I made out the 75-48 Police Report and made an entry on my Patrol Log. As soon as I informed the Police Communications Unit that I was available for assignment, I was given an assignment of a "loud party" at a residence on McKean Street just south of Queen Lane. This was a short distance away. Normally, "loud party" assignments were given to a one-person unit. Because such assignments may quickly become disturbances, another vehicle would usually take the initiative to ride in on the assignment, but remain available for other calls. In this instance, Emergency Patrol Wagon 1402 never came back into service from our disturbance call and rode in with me to the "loud party" assignment. It was approximately 1:30am on a Sunday morning. As I arrived to the assignment, I found the residence dark and quiet. All of the surrounding residences were dark and quiet. Standing at the door and window of the residence for a few minutes, I could hear neither music nor conversation. In less than five minutes, I determined that the assignment was unfounded. There was no need to knock at the door and possibly awake sleeping people. I, immediately, put myself back into service and made myself available for another assignment. I was often criticized for putting myself back into service immediately after an assignment was completed. Department policy allowed for thirty minutes per assignment unless extenuating circumstances required a longer time. Many veteran Officers would take advantage of this policy and linger out of service just to take a break. I hated that practice. I enjoyed my work. After I put myself in service from this "loud party" assignment, 1402 wagon went back into service. On my

*Police Incident Report #75-48 and my written-in-ink Patrol
Log, I noted that 1402 wagon assisted me, even though they
did not go out of service for the assignment. I thought this
would be the end of that assignment.*

*In late September or early October, I came in to work the "Last
Out" shift. It was a week night. After Roll Call, my Sergeant
told me that I had to report to the Internal Affairs Bureau
at 319 Race Street, immediately. This was shocking. This
meant I was in some kind of trouble. No one goes to Internal
Affairs unless they have been accused to doing something
wrong. I had never been there before. Normally, all business
at Internal Affairs was handled during day time hours. The
Sergeant could not give me a reason for my having to go there.
After I arrived, I sat down for an interview with two Staff
Inspectors. They began to question me about the "loud party"
assignment on McKean Street. At first, I could not remember
the assignment. They showed me my ink written patrol log
and a copy of my 75-48. Now, I remembered. Then, I was
able to accurately describe what happened just prior to and
during this assignment. As my interview concluded, the Staff
Inspectors informed me that this investigation was among
several of this type they were investigating. Members and
sympathizers of the Black Panther Party had filed several
complaints about abuse of power by Police Officers. So far,
all of the complaints were unsubstantiated. In the complaint
against me about the "loud party", the complainants stated
that I came into the residence and that I spoke in a loud
and profane manner to the occupants of the house. The
complaint stated that while in the residence, I punctuated
my verbal behavior by knocking over some furniture items
and warning the occupants that if returned, I would arrest
everyone in the house. The complainants stated that I was the
only responding Police Officer. They stated that I remained in
the house for approximately thirty minutes. I must note that
the Black Panther Party had a store-front office a few yards*

away in the 400 block of West Queen Lane. Because of the information written in ink on my Patrol log, and because of their replaying of taped Police Radio conversations they were able to clearly establish that I was back in service and responding to other assignments during the time that the Black Panther Party accusers stated that I was at their residence. Those accusers had no idea that Emergency Patrol Wagon 1402 had responded to the assignment. Perhaps, a week after my interview, I received notification that this investigation showed the accusation of misconduct was unfounded. It was a fraudulent attempt to misrepresent Police behavior. For the remainder of my career as a Police Officer, I filled out my Patrol Logs in ink. This was a small, but important success story for me.) Now, we can move back in time.

Part of the duties of a Police Officer on the "Last Out" shift included Club Checks at 3:00am. While regular bars or taverns had to close at 2:00am, "Social Clubs" with a license to sell alcohol could stay open until 3:00am. At that time, Police Officers had to check each club to insure that no drinks were being served after 3:00am. Ideally, the Officer was supposed to stay until all customers had left the premises. This could take a long time for some of the more popular clubs. Some sectors had one club. Some unfortunate Officers had two or more social clubs. Couple that with the fact that 3:00am on weekends was a busy time. In those days, Police Officers did not have portable radios. Once you were out of your police vehicle, you were out of contact with your radio.

On this particular first night, my partner and I had to make a Club Check at a social club located at Wissahickon Ave., and Manheim St. There were many cars in the driveway. As we pulled into the driveway, the veteran Officer asked, "Kid, do you take a note?" A "note" is money given to an Officer by a civilian to encourage that Officer to ignore illegal activity. First of all, I remember this practice from Police Officers on Harlan St., my childhood home. Secondly, our training at the Police Academy told us that this was prohibitive behavior. My rapid response to the question was "No, I don't believe in that." He responded, "Okay, wait in the car. Do not answer the radio. I'll be back." He notified Police Radio that we would be out of service making a Club Check. This was against normal practice for a two-person car. Perhaps, he did not trust this rookie to respond to calls. I sat there for thirty-minutes. When he returned, most of the same cars we saw at the beginning were still there. As he walked to the car, he stuffed something into his pants pocket. I assumed it was money. We left and drove to the district to turn in a report on the "club closing".

I was developing a bad impression about veteran Police Officers. As we returned to riding down cobblestoned Germantown Ave., my soul was being rattled. It was not just because of the bumpy ride but also because of the bumpy behavior I was experiencing. Were all Police Officers like this? Unlike when I walked a beat, security checks were done cursory manner. You did not get out of your vehicle, you just checked the exterior windows. I found that this type of laziness was the norm and not the exception. Almost everyone made club checks the same way. Almost everyone patrolled the same way. I was determined not to let this behavior taint me. I could barely wait until I had an opportunity to work alone. I was here to suppress crime and to make the community better. These cops were just collecting a paycheck and a little extra on the side. This was not far from what my Academy mates had told me while attending a party a few weeks prior to this. Still, it was alarming to see it up close.

What I did not know at the time was that my refusal to "take a note" was passed on to the entire squad by the next day. By the end of the week, I was back walking the beat on Germantown Ave. I was an instant outsider. I was disappointed, but determined. By the second week, the foot beat seemed to be my normal assignment. That only changed if someone had a day off or called off sick. If that person worked an Emergency Patrol Wagon, I would be the recorder (report writer) on the wagon as that vehicle had to be operated by two Police Officers. Again, I was told not to answer the radio. I had to record in pencil and follow the instructions of the senior officer. I was beginning to prefer walking on a foot beat.

During my second week, we were working the 4pm – 12am shift. While working this shift, I introduced myself to many of the merchants. They were all happy to see a Police Officer walking outside of their businesses. This was what I wanted. One veteran officer told me that walking a beat was much more preferable than driving a police car. His reasons were that you established community contact and you did not have to respond to radio calls. I was enjoying the community contact.

By my third week, working the day shift, I had an opportunity to work alone in a radio patrol car. It was exciting. Day shift presented this opportunity because on the day shift many Officers had to attend court. Their patrol duties had to be covered because most sectors had school crossings that had to be covered by a uniformed Officer. Covering these crossings reminded me of my elementary school days. While in the 4th grade, I became a member of the Safety Patrol. This meant I covered school crossings with a Crossing Guard. There were normally six to eight "Safeties" per corner. By the 6th grade, I was promoted to Captain of the Safety Patrol. This meant that I arranged assignments and filled in when other "Safeties" were absent. I had no idea at that time, that fourteen years in the future, I would be doing those same duties as a Police Officer.

Working the day shift presented different challenges than the other shifts. One had to make a security checks of all banks and companies which handled large amounts of money. Each bank had to be checked a minimum of twice per tour. This was a good thing because I had to park the vehicle, walk into the bank, and sign a security log. This gave me an opportunity to check other businesses and interact with more people. There was always the tension of a possible encounter with a bank robber or a disruptive person in a business. Day shift was very busy but usually not the same type of busy one encountered on the 4pm – 12am shift. Most of all, I enjoyed working alone. I did not have to tolerate the bad behavior of veteran Officers. I could work the way I had been taught at the Police Academy. I was focused on serving the public in the best way possible and I was always looking for the bad guys. I learned later that finding bad guys was a combination of both skill and luck.

After that first week of day shift, I found myself once again walking a foot beat on most nights of the Last Out shift. This was beginning to be frustrating. After all, in Task Force, I never walked a beat. I was spoiled. What were they holding against me? I came to work prepared. My uniform was always spotless. After about three months of what I considered less than first class treatment, I decided to apply for a transfer. I knew I could not go back to the Task Force Unit. I decided to apply for a transfer to the elite Highway Patrol Division. There, I would be riding in a vehicle and focused on crime suppression. The Highway Patrol Division was normally assigned to high crime areas. Very little of their duty involved patrolling Philadelphia's only two highways, i.e., the Schuylkill Expressway (Interstate 76) and the Delaware Expressway (Interstate 95).

Part of my transfer request asked for my reason for seeking this transfer. As I had been taught at the US Military Academy Preparatory School, I wrote my honest answer. I cited my desire to focus on crime. I stated that many Officers in my district avoided becoming involved in either suppressing crime or apprehending criminals. I noted that many came to work with wrinkled uniforms and appeared to be physically unfit for the rigors of aggressive patrol duties. A week after I turned in my transfer, my Platoon Lieutenant hailed me after the 4pm – 12am Roll Call.

As I approached him, he stated, "You've got a lot of guts turning in this transfer." His eyes were glaring. His tone was offensive. My heart was pounding. I was almost speechless. "Who do you think you are, writing this crap in a transfer?" I told him, "I was just writing how I felt." I am sure I must have sounded sheepish. He then stated that the District Captain wanted to speak with me. The Captain had recently been assigned to our district. The 14th Police District had been cited for having the most frequent occurrences of police brutality complaints. The strong rumor was that the Police Department was pressured into bringing in a new Commander. This new Commanding Officer was tasked with lowering the incidence of these complaints.

This Captain had been transferred from North Philly's 22nd Police District. He did not have a smile on his face when I entered his office. He wanted to know why I wanted to transfer to the Highway Patrol Division. I quoted to him all of my aforementioned reasons. He stated that he and most District Captains had a low opinion of the Highway Patrol Division. He stated that the best quality of Police Officers worked in the districts. They were more versatile and more in tune to what was going on in the community. After all of his compliments for district Officers, his real agenda surfaced. "I have read this transfer and Norman, if I forward this transfer as you have written it, we will have Staff Inspectors here for every Roll Call." He indicated the Staff Inspectors would be going through records and riding around the district trying to find Officers misbehaving. He stated that he would not allow that.

"Staff Inspectors" were a newly created rank. They were ranked between Captains and full Inspectors. All were assigned to the Police Internal Affairs Bureau. Their duty was to investigate all instances of police misconduct and to recommend either disciplinary action or to find that no infraction had been committed. District Commanders feared them because they knew that these Inspectors might find something that could damage their careers. My Captain sternly looked at me. He stated, "If you want to go to Highway, just rewrite this transfer. In the reason section, just put that you would like to try out in this unit." He stated that he had friends in Highway Patrol and he would do whatever he could to approve the transfer. He handed me back the transfer. I indicated that I would comply with his request. I left his office shaken and angry. I wasn't trying to cause a problem. I just wanted to get out of this district. I was hesitant to rewrite the transfer. I did not trust the Captain. My intuition told me that he was less than honest when he stated that he would help me in transferring to the Highway Patrol Division. I knew that there were worst assignments than the 14th Police District. I tore up the transfer request and decided to cast my lot with the "devil I knew."

As a result of the resentment by Supervisors of my transfer request, I found myself being assigned to a large amount of details that required me to travel outside of my district. These were details such as riding with a team from the Society for the Prevention of Cruelty to Animals as they drove through different neighborhoods picking up stray dogs. This detail happened almost every day work tour. Also on the day shift, I was often assigned to the Subway Detail. This unpleasant detail required that I come to work at my normal time then leave at approximately 12:00pm to report to the Police Department's Subway Unit by 1:30pm. This detail had Officers assigned to ride Philadelphia's subway and elevated trains in order to deter bad behavior from school students. Most school students were respectful but there were always a few who wanted to either fight gang battles or harass passengers who were either adults or children who attended schools other than theirs. It was a necessary detail, but it was very inconvenient for the eighteen to twenty officers who reported for this detail every weekday.

These two details paled to the other stupid assignments I was frequently given. On the 4pm – 12pm and 12pm – 8pm tours the Police Department maintained a "Bus Detail". The objective was to have a contingent of Police Officers available to respond to emergency situations throughout the city. On the 4pm – 12am shift, all Officers on this detail would be assigned to a North Broad Street Detail. Broad Street extended the entire width of Philadelphia. It was six driving lanes wide with a center median strip. Under normal circumstances three lanes each are assigned to both northbound and southbound traffic during the morning and evening rush hours. During the evening rush hour, one southbound lane was flexed into a northbound lane. For 56 city blocks, a Police Officer had to stand on the medial strip at every major intersection north of City Hall (Center City).

We did not direct traffic. We were living blue totem poles. Ideally, we were to assist pedestrians who were crossing the street who might become confused because of the extra lane assigned to northbound traffic. In rainy weather, you were soaked by not only the falling rain, but by drivers who saw this as an opportunity to speed up and splash water on a defenseless stationary cop. During cold weather, one's feet would become numb and one's leg joints would stiffen. This detail ran from 4pm – 6pm every day. It did not take me long to realize that speaking out had its penalties in the Police Department. The details were supposed to rotate among all Officers within a squad. Some Officers were never assigned to them. Someone such as I would be assigned to these details an inordinate amount of times. This was the beginning of the socialization of a Police Officer. This was the foundation of the "wall of silence". This was how the department muted dissent. At this point in time, I had no idea that the behavior I was experiencing was a microcosm of things to come.

After several weeks, I was finally assigned a "steady car". The Police Officer who was normally assigned to Radio Patrol Car (RPC) 143 had been wounded in a robbery attempt at a supermarket on Germantown Ave. Until his return, his car would be my assignment. The sector for this car was the southwestern corner of the 14th District. This area was in the midst of a change from working class Caucasians to working class African Americans. It was not long before I made my first arrest in this area.

While monitoring a midday school crossing at the intersection of Green and Logan Streets, a pedestrian informed me that there were two men fighting in the courtyard of St. Francis of Assisi Church. Via Police Radio, I requested assistance and I went to investigate the complaint. As

I entered the courtyard, I observed two middle aged men engaged in a struggle. I could clearly see blood. As I approached the men, I could clearly see that one male was repeatedly stabbing the other in the chest. I did the best I could to pull the two men apart. The man on top was yelling at the other in Italian. After failing to pull them apart, I drew my revolver and placed it near the face of the aggressor. Now, I had his attention. He relaxed and I took the bloody switch blade knife from him. Soon, other Officers arrived. We arrested the stabber and the victim was taken to Germantown Hospital.

Needless to say, my adrenalin rush had me shaking with excitement. I had possibly saved a life in my first arrest under violent circumstances. Surely, this might lead to my first court trial. Such would not be the case. What would become a far too familiar practice occurred at the Preliminary Hearing held the following week. To my surprise, both men appeared at the hearing. At that time, the Attorney for the stabber revealed that the men were cousins. Both men had recently moved to the United States from Italy. They had a long simmering feud that culminated in the event in which I had intervened. Through a lawyer, the victim told the Assistant District Attorney that he did not want to prosecute his cousin. All charges were dismissed. Both the victim and the perpetrator walked out together. I was in disbelief. A veteran Officer explained to me that this was the reason you do not get personally involved with arrests. He told me that I would see this scenario repeated frequently in court. He was 100% correct. I did see this scenario repeated especially in domestic abuse cases. This was the reason most Police Officers did not like to get involved with domestic abuse assignments. Often, the abused woman would attack the Police Officers if they attempted to arrest the male abuser. It seemed that in ninety percent of domestic abuse cases, the female would fail to appear at the preliminary hearing and the charges would be dismissed. I had a classic case of this two years after this incident.

On an autumn Thursday night, I was assigned to guard a store front whose display window had been broken. It was about 9:00pm. The location was on cobblestoned Germantown Avenue about 50 yards north of Wister St. At Germantown and Wister a popular tavern was packed with joyous patrons. After about thirty minutes into my assignment, a male and female left the tavern. They were having a profanity laced argument. The male began to slap and punch the woman. She tried to fight back, but the best she could do was scream for "help" as he pummeled her with overpowering punches. I intervened and used my portable radio to call for assistance. As the Emergency Patrol Wagon arrived, I told the male, who was the husband of the woman, that I was placing him under arrest for assault. The woman became livid. "We had a murder around here last night. Why don't you look for the murderer instead of bothering my husband?" After several minutes of her insisting that she would not press charges against her husband, I elected to release the male. There was no sense in burdening the system with another domestic abuse case that would result in charges being dropped. About two hours after this incident, I was driving south on Germantown Ave. on my way home from work. I saw the husband face down on the sidewalk outside of the tavern at Germantown and Wister. A quick investigation revealed that the couple returned to the tavern and the male resumed assaulting his wife. An "unknown" male in the tavern became angered by the husband's behavior and knocked him unconscious. It seemed as though the battering coward had received his just reward.

That women would tolerate a severe battering by a man has always left me puzzled.

> *I saw this type of battering occur in my own household as I grew up. I detested it. I learned to despise any man who would beat a woman. What did it ever prove? Did these men brag to their friends about how well their wives could take a punch in the face? Did they feel more masculine when they kicked their wives in their stomachs? My police career had revealed to me that men who believe in beating their female companion/wife were usually on the low end of the courage scale. They would cry like babies when placed in a holding cell. Yes, they were normally the cowards of our society. Still, some women would find a way to perpetually forgive these Neanderthals.*

Not too long after my somewhat permanent assignment to Radio Patrol Car 143, I learned the unnerving truth about accurate crime reporting. One spring evening, I received an assignment to go to a residence in the

200 block of West Hansberry St. An African American male wanted to report that his car was stolen. His vehicle was a car he owned for about six years. I filled out the very detailed Stolen Auto Report and went directly into headquarters. I was excited. This was my first "Stolen Auto Report". I walked into the Operations Room and turned my report over to the Corporal. "This is not a stolen car, this is a "Try and Locate", he gruffly stated. I countered that the man knew that he parked his car in front of his house and when he checked for it in the evening, it was missing. Condescendingly, the Corporal looked at me and told me that when a car is over five years old, it is never entered into the crime reports as a "stolen vehicle". It is always entered into the reporting system as a "Try and Locate" (actual classification).

This was alarming to me. I took it as a purposeful slap in the face of all low income people who could not afford a new car. Of course, because of my limited experience at the time, I assumed there had to be a racial context to this. I learned that this was a practice not only, in the 14th Police District but throughout the Police Department. This practice requires some explanation to give those not experienced in police practices. While at the Police Academy, we were taught that when a vehicle is placed in "Try and Locate" status, it means that the owner forgot where he parked the vehicle. Also, it could mean that a teenager drove the vehicle, had an accident, but did not want to give his parents the location. It was not a crime. The vehicle would be placed in the Philadelphia Crime Information Computer System (PCIC), but not entered into the National Crime Information Computer System (NCIC). During this period, the Police Department did not have the sophisticated computer system of the latter part of the 20th Century. When a Police Officer began his shift, he would pick up two sheets of paper. The first sheet was the "Part One Sheet". This sheet was a report of all "Part One" crimes that occurred during the previous day. "Part One" crimes are felonies (the most serious crimes) that the Federal Bureau of Investigation tracks via its Uniform Crime Reporting System. This was a national tracking system that monitored crime trends throughout the country. The second sheet an Officer picked up was the "Stolen Vehicle Sheet". This was a mimeographed sheet that was circulated city-wide. On one side of the sheet under the heading "Stolen Vehicle", were the vehicle registration tags of all vehicles reported stolen or wanted for crimes in Philadelphia. On the other side of the sheet under the heading "Try and Locate" was a list of the vehicle registration tags of all vehicles that were "lost" by the owners. Both sides of this sheet contained about 250 registration tags. It is important to note that for the twenty-five years of my career, this was the practice. Therefore, there were a thousands of stolen vehicles that were never recorded by the Philadelphia Police Department as stolen.

If an unauthorized person were apprehended driving a vehicle listed in "Try and Locate" status, a convoluted process would begin. The arresting Police Officer would take the person to the appropriate Detective Division. The assigned Detective would change the status of the vehicle from "Try and Locate" to "Stolen". This meant the status was changed from a non-criminal incident to a major felony arrest. The fractured thinking behind this process was that unsolved crimes reflect poorly on the department and the city. If you cleared a crime by an arrest, that made the city look as if it had an efficient Police Department. Unfortunately, this arrest process would only occur if the vehicle and operator were apprehended in Philadelphia. If the same event occurred outside of Philadelphia, it would be impossible of a Police Officer to immediately determine that the vehicle was stolen. This was the negative impact of a Police Department doing its best to hide relevant crime statistics from its citizens. This practice existed for decades.

It was not until I had an entry in the Letters to the Editor section of the Philadelphia Daily News in 1997 that this practice was revealed. Only after my appearance on the Dateline NBC television program in 1998 was this practice stopped. Up until that time, stolen vehicle tags were always reported as lost and older vehicles would always be reported as "Try and Locate". This allowed the Police Commissioner and the Mayor to boast about how their policies were lowering the crime rate, when all the time they were fighting crime with an eraser. While a Police Officer and Police Corporal, I complained about this to the Fraternal Order of Police. I viewed this as the government's way to justify lowering the number of Police Officers on the patrol. The Fraternal Order of Police, the bargaining agent for all Police Officers in Philadelphia was not interested in pursuing this issue. So much for Honor, Integrity and Service (the Police Department's motto). I could not understand why a bargaining agent for Police Officers that was supposedly concerned about the safety of its membership would not challenge a policy that was used to decrease the number of Police Officers on patrol.

On the evening of April 4, 1968, I was driving in my personal vehicle when I heard that Reverend Dr. Martin Luther King had been assassinated. This was devastating news. This champion of civil rights was one of the most respected men in the world. He had won the Nobel Peace Prize in 1964. At a time when there was an aggressive campaign to gain voting rights for African Americans in the southern portion of the United States, the acknowledged leader of the American Civil Rights Movement had been slain. Because of irresponsible threats from 2nd tier African American leaders such as Stokely Carmichael, H. Rap Brown, and Huey Newton there was a great fear that anger over the murder of Rev. Dr. King would lead to Rioting in African-American Communities throughout America. These "leaders", whose followers could not distinguish reality from rhetoric, had their wishes realized. Immediately, after the news of the assassination was announced, these irresponsible media parasites gained enough access to radio and television to call for African Americans to "retaliate" for the assassination by burning up their neighborhoods. Major urban areas that had significant African American populations throughout American began to erupt in rioting.

I found it odd that the very people who encouraged the rioting held Reverend Martin Luther King in disdain. At the news of his murder, they called for African Americans to engage in the very behavior that Rev. Dr. King taught was non-productive. I and every Police Officer knew that the following day, all of us would be working extended shifts. These extended shifts over a long periods of time disrupted the family life of every Police Officer. In the late 1960's and early 1970's Philadelphia Police Officers were always prepared for a "long hot summer" of racial tension and extended shifts.

On Friday, April 5, 1968, I reported for work at 8:00am. At that time we were told that our shifts would be extended until, at least, 8:00pm. All Police Officers would be working twelve-hour shifts until further notice. I was wondering with whom I had to work for twelve hours in a police car. There was no way, I wanted to work with a lazy, coffee drinking, assignment dodging partner for twelve hours. I should have been careful what I wished for.

I was assigned to "14 Foot Beat 5." That was twelve hours working on a foot beat. There were no portable radios at that time. "14 Foot Beat 5" was a special beat in our district. This beat was located in a predominantly African American neighborhood (oddly called Pulaski Town). The only purpose for the beat was to guard "Cranes Tavern." Cranes Tavern was a popular place for high profile politicians to meet. This relatively small tavern was located next to the sixteen storied Queen Lane Apartments. This Public Housing Project contained 119 apartments which housed impoverished African American families. As with most housing projects it was a crime haven. The surrounding neighborhood was composed of two and three storied houses. The customers at "Cranes Tavern" were predominantly middle to high income Caucasian people. When Police Officers were not in the area, these customers were frequently assault and robbery victims. Because former Mayor James H. J. Tate and several other high local government officials frequented this establishment, this foot beat was deemed a priority foot beat. Coverage of this beat was mandatory between the hours of 5pm and 1am. It was deemed as a choice assignment because the owners of Cranes "loved a cop." They were known to provide the Police Officer assigned to the beat with a good free meal. In addition, at the end of the week the Officer would receive a free bottle of liquor and $5.00. The Sergeant would receive $5.00. This was not a secret. Everyone knew about it. Despite the beat being located in a predominantly African American neighborhood, African American Police Officers were never assigned to the beat. This was simply because of the "benefits" of being assigned to the beat.

Oddly enough, assaults and robberies were diminished but they did not stop. The Officers assigned to this beat were the same lazy, coffee drinking, assignment dodging Officers I had grown to dislike. In my mind, they were just sponges soaking up food and money while doing the minimum amount of work. There were never any arrests of note made by these Officers. On April 5, 1968, "14 Foot Beat #5" became my twelve-hour assignment for a significant portion of the spring and summer seasons. Did I mention that I am African American? Did I mention that no African American Police Officer had ever been assigned to this beat?

Now, that there was a fear of rioting by angry, misled African American criminals (usually the only ones rioting), there arose a need to place an African American sacrificial lamb in the midst of chaos to appease the community.

I was angry. I was slightly familiar with the area. "We are not to wonder why. We are just to do and die." Maybe, I would only have this assignment for a day or two. Maybe, African American minds would catch up to the 20th Century and see that tearing up the neighborhoods in which they lived was not the way to deal with affronts to our culture. I quickly learned that my thoughts were not the thoughts of my kinsmen. There were riots all over the country. Philadelphia was tense, but there were no riots. No-nonsense, bellicose Police Commissioner Frank L. Rizzo was proactive in maintaining a heavy police presence in areas with predominantly African American populations. Most police vehicles had a minimum of two and often three Police Officers. Any type of disturbance call resulted in an overwhelming presence of nervous Police Officers. Nervous and fearful Police Officers in tense situations can be a catalyst for disaster. I took this assignment as a corporate slap in the face. No African-American Police Officer was good enough to work this assignment during normal times. A perceived threat was enough to remove Caucasian Officers from this "lucrative" foot beat. They were cowards.

One proactive measure the Police Commissioner issued was an order to curtail riotous activity. It was a proclamation that no groups larger than five people were allowed to congregate anywhere in the city. Okay, I am in a predominantly Afro-American neighborhood, with a fully occupied 16-storied Public Housing Apartment Building, next to a playground with basketball courts and I am single-handedly supposed to maintain crowd control. Cranes Restaurant at Priscilla St. and Queen Lane did not open for business. The young men of the Housing Project decided that this would be a good place to congregate. Perhaps, they had an idea to break into this tavern and steal items from inside. I had to be discreet and appeal to their better nature to encourage them not to assemble on this corner. I encouraged them to meet in the playground. I suggested to them that no Police Officer was going to bother them if they were on or near the basketball court. Reluctantly, they heeded my suggestion. I knew that I felt that I would have to work among these young men for several days. It would be best that I established a friendly rapport with them and give to them a viable option to standing on this corner. I solved the problem by making it "my" corner. No one wanted to hang out on a corner where a cop was standing. No one ever relieved me to take a break. I had to remain on this beat and stand in almost the same spot for twelve hours.

At this time, no Police Officer had a portable radio. My only communication with the Police Department would be via pay telephones one block away at either Morris St., and Queen Lane or Penn St. and Pulaski Ave. As nerve wracking as it was, this was the beginning of my learning how to deal with street thugs. Yes, time proved that most of these guys were thugs. But my first interaction with them was to treat them as honest young men. No cussing. No threats of arrest. "Hey guys, this is a bad time for all of us. We can all have an easy night if you assemble somewhere else, like the playground. No one is going to bother you there. I won't bother you there. You just cannot hang out here or on any street corner." Words of this type seemed to diffuse some of their normal resistance to requests by Police Officers. Unfortunately, I found myself on this beat for a very long time. For the first several days, Cranes Tavern did not open. After the business opened, I did little else but stand near the place. Every once in a while, I would check other businesses on my beat which extended five blocks from Wayne Ave, to the Wissahickon Train Station. Because, I knew I could not stay away too long, I seldom walked to the Wissahickon Train Station after dark. As a result, I never had a robbery or assault take place while I was on that beat. It seemed as though every 4pm – 12am shift and 12pm – 8am shift, I found myself assigned to work from 5pm – 1am on 14 Foot Beat #5.

Although, I first resented it, I had an opportunity to acquaint myself with some of the better people in that area. I seldom went into the restaurant to eat. In fact, after several weeks, a Manager walked out and nearly pulled me inside in order to give me a meal. The staff there was very appreciative of my always being somewhere near the business. Still, I seldom went in to eat and I made it clear that I would not take any money nor any liquor. I was doing my job and making a salary. That was enough for me.

It was a bit irritating to me and the management of the tavern when during my second week, a District Operations crew sent an Emergency Patrol Wagon to Cranes and ordered 14 sandwiches for Police Officers who were afraid to come down to my beat to check on my well-being. Of course, there was no offer to pay for the sandwiches. The staff had to make those sandwiches and prepare food for the customers in the tavern. Disgraceful behavior that I would see repeated many times during my tenure in the 14th Police District. It was embarrassing.

Please do not entertain the idea that all was pleasant on this beat. Remember, only a few other Officers, normally African American Officers, ever took the time to check on me while I was on this beat. On Sunday, April 7, 1968, I discovered how bad it could become. I was working the 8am – 8pm shift. I was standing at the corner of Morris St. and Queen Lane when a nun from a nearby Catholic Rectory breathlessly approached me. She had run two- blocks to tell me that a man was disrupting services at her church, St. Catherine's. As she talked, we walked towards the church. Soon, she pointed to the disruptive male who was a block away from us walking east on Penn St. from Morris St. I clearly knew that this was an indication the problem was over, but still, I needed to talk to the male. I caught up with him at Penn St. and Pulaski Ave. This was the corner where there were about fifty young men playing or watching basketball in the playground.

As I began to talk to the male, he responded by punching me in the face. This 5'6", 130 pound dynamo was high on some narcotic. He almost caused me to fall as we struggled. I knew that if I fell, I would likely get stomped on by the nearby crowd. Eventually, I was able to control him with a half-nelson hold (an arm around his neck). I pulled him to a nearby telephone and attempted to call for help. This was difficult at the time. I had to hold him while reaching into my pocket to find a dime. Then, I had to put the dime into the small coin slot and dial the telephone. I was at a huge disadvantage.

The Little Dynamo broke away and ran diagonally to the southeast corner of Penn St. and Pulaski Ave. I was able to apprehend and hold him. When I turned around, I was surrounded by all fifty of the young men who were in the playground. One of the men, who was about 30 years old, demanded that I release Little Dynamo. I told him, that I would not. He stated that if I did not release him, then "we will take him from you." I assured him that if the crowd attempted to take him from me, then he would be the first person I would come after.

In reality, the crowd was pressed so close to us that it was impossible for me to draw either my baton or my revolver. I had to maintain some sense of calm and hope that help would come. After what seemed like an eternity, all of us could hear police sirens approaching the location. I found out that a passerby notified Police Officers several blocks away that an Officer was in trouble. The crowd dispersed. I arrested the male. After completing all of the necessary paperwork, I returned to the same beat. As usual, I was there alone. Of course, my reason for going back to the beat was because no one wanted to be in that neighborhood after a Police Officer had made an arrest. My returning to the beat was not a matter of punishment, but a means of survival for all of the sandwich grabbing-assignment dodging Officers working with me. This is not an indictment against all of the Officers, just the Caucasian Officers who wanted to get the sandwiches, the five dollars, and the bottle of liquor while not giving a damn about protecting the community.

Now, the thugs seemed to have hardened their attitude towards me. I could no longer be "Officer Friendly" to them. They hated that I had arrested one of their "Black brothers." The truth was, Little Dynamo was a drug addict who did not live in the area. Our relationship was never the same after that. Not a problem. I think they respected that I came right back to the beat rather than hide. I knew from my North Philly upbringing that once you showed fear you would rapidly become a victim. When in doubt, act crazy. No one wants to deal with a crazy person, especially a crazy cop. At 5'10" and 153 pounds, I was not going to cast an intimidating shadow in this community. Still, I was a bit disappointed in these thugs of the Pulaski Town community. I came on the job to protect people from bad behavior. Here they were turning against me in a way that my North Philadelphia community would never have done. Police Officers were respected and feared in my neighborhood. Taking a prisoner away from them was unthinkable. I had to find other means to relate and get my job done. I think I wore out my 24-hour deodorant by the sixth hour of every working day on this beat.

After several weeks, I was awarded my first steady car. Radio Patrol Car 146 would be my steady assignment. Unfortunately, this car's sector included the Queen Lane beat. After my assignment to this car, the "in-crowd" of Police Officers began to tell me all of the places to "pick up a note", i.e. a small amount of money to ignore illegal activity. I made it clear that I wanted no part of it.

About a month after I received this steady assignment, I ran into my first challenge from a Police Officer. One of the radio patrol cars that adjoined my sector was that of RPC 148. On this particular Friday evening, RPC 148 was not operating due to a mechanical problem. As was the normal procedure, the Officer on that car would double up with an Officer on an adjoining car if a replacement car was not available. Officer Timbers (not his true name) teamed up with me that evening. He was a seasoned Officer with a few years of experience. I drove. He recorded. That suited him fine. About 8:00pm, we were slowly cruising west bound in the 200 block of West Coulter St. "There's our vice pinch (arrest)" he yelled as he pointed to a middle-age African American male walking on the south side of the street. This was an experienced Officer. Excitedly, I responded, "What did he do? Do you know him?" I was not ready for his response. "Nah, the way it works is, we pick him up, write a few numbers on a piece of paper, and slip it in his pocket. We get a vice pinch (for illegal lottery) and make the Sergeant happy." Now, I was in *MY* car. This was *MY* sector and this veteran was trying to get *ME* to go along with something immoral and illegal. I was incensed.

"I don't work that way", I answered angrily. "I grew up in a neighborhood where cops did that type of thing all the time. I promised that I would never do that. We are not going to arrest this man. He's not doing anything but walking home."

Timbers was silent. My adrenalin was up for the entire night. We finished our shift without exchanging too many words. The next night, RPC 148 was still out of service, but Timbers worked with another Officer. I worked alone. For the remainder of my tenure in the 14th Police District, I seldom worked with an experienced Officer. I would only be partnered with rookie, i.e. newer officers. The word was out. I did not take money. I did not make bogus arrests. I wanted a broad line drawn between cops and robbers. At this time, I had no idea that I would again be presented with this challenge in a more horrific way in the future. Once again, I was reminded of my self-promise to end this type of behavior in the African American (Black) Community. I was not going to allow peer pressure to change me. Integrity was important to me.

A few months after my assignment to RPC 146, I would receive another example of how much the Black Community appreciated having a concerned Black Police Officer in their community. I was working the 8am- 4pm shift on a sunny July weekday. I received a call to meet the Manager of a bank located in the 200 block of West Chelten Ave. On my arrival, the Manager directed me to his desk where an elderly Caucasian woman was sitting. She had come to the bank to withdraw $10,000 from her savings account. She stated that she had been contacted by an "Internal Revenue Agent" who was investigating fraudulent activity with her bank account. After speaking to her by telephone, the "Agent" met with her. The "Agent" stated that this woman needed to withdraw a large amount of money from her account in order to trap the "offender". After obtaining the money, the "Agent" would hold the money until their investigation was completed. At the end of the investigation, the money would be returned to her account. This happened to be a frequent scam that the Bank Teller immediately recognized. The Bank Teller notified her Manager, who in turn called the Police Department. The woman was able to give me a perfect description of the two "Agents" with whom she spoke. In fact, she was able to point them out to me. They were two African-American women. I could see them through the large bank window.

From the bank, I called the Police Communications Unit and asked for a back-up officer. I had to use a telephone because Police Officers did not have portable radios. Because I feared the women might take flight. I went to detain them. Both women were about 35 – 40 years of age. I confronted them on the sidewalk and attempted to engage them in conversation about their reason for standing outside of the bank. Both began to protest my questioning in extremely loud voices. Their voice level was out of context with my conversation. This behavior assured me that they were not at this location for honorable reasons. "Why (sic) you questioning us? We a'int do nothin'", they protested. They were loud and animated. Within seconds a large crowd from this busy shopping district began to surround me. All of those surrounding me were African American adults. The vocal ones in the crowd began to echo the protestations of the female suspects. Some men in the crowd pulled the women away from me and others formed a barrier between me and the women. Just recently, on July 15, 1968, Police Officer Ross Brackett was killed after an assailant took the Officer's gun and shot him with it. This was my first concern as the crowd pressed around me. I did not draw my revolver, but I kept my right forearm pressed against it so that I could feel if someone tried to grab it. The women were escorted to a nearby vehicle and they fled the scene. As others warned that another police vehicle was approaching, the crowd rapidly dispersed.

Once again, the community I had sworn and self-promised to protect turned against me for trying to place criminals under arrest. This was beginning to look like a dangerous trend. The idiots in the crowd were emboldened by a new trend to challenge Police Officers who were arresting any African-American. The seed for this trend was planted during the Philadelphia "Race Riot" of 1964 and by "Race Riots" in other cities. None of these riots had anything to do with racial injustices. These riots were acts of vandalism and violence that would be more accurately characterized as crimes of opportunity. They were masked as righteous indignation due to past and current instances of racial injustice. In addition, during the years from 1966 to 1976 there were violent Black Militant groups who threatened to kill Police Officers. They were not unique during that time as several predominantly Caucasian groups swore to kill law enforcement Officers. The women in this incident escaped and were never caught. At least, the elderly woman kept her $10,000.

I learned a lot in the 14th Police District. In busy districts, you have to learn quickly. I remember responding to a late night call in the 6800 block of Chew Avenue. It was a disturbance call. There was a male threatening a female with a knife. I was about the sixth Police Officer to respond. On my arrival, the man with the knife was in a 2nd Floor bedroom. He threatened to stab any police Officer who attempted to arrest him. I, reached for my pistol. A veteran Officer touched my hand signaling for me not to do anything. One Officer, Johnny J. calmly talked to the man. As Johnny J. talked, another Officer positioned himself so that he could use his baton to knock the knife from the man's hand. The male was arrested without injury to anyone. This was a good lesson learned. I was proud of my team. They had done an admirable job. This was a lesson I would carry with me throughout my career. Just because a disturbed person was holding a knife, you did not have to respond with deadly force if other means of disarming him/her are readily and safely available.

Outstanding Events in the 14th Police District

On the Saturday evening of July 4th weekend (July 6) in 1968, I was working the 12am – 8am shift in RPC 146. I was just leaving the District Headquarters at about 1:30am, when an Officer, I shall call Officer Kelly, called over the radio to ask for an Emergency Patrol Wagon (EPW) to transport an intoxicated female he was detaining at Germantown and Mt. Airy Aves. Unfortunately, we had no wagons available in the 14th District. After several calls for EPW's, the Police Radio Dispatcher instructed EPW 502 from the 5th Police District to respond. This was a considerable distance for the wagon to come. It would mean a several minute wait for the Officer and that is never a good thing. I decided to go the location to assist him.

Normal procedure for transporting a prisoner if there is no wagon available was to place the prisoner in the rear seat of the vehicle and have another vehicle closely follow. I notified Police Radio, that I was on my way to Germantown and Mt. Airy Aves. It was a 13 block ride to the location. The wheels of my RPC hummed as I rode over the rough cobblestones of Germantown Ave. Three-quarters of my way to the assignment, Officer Kelly spoke over the radio, "Resume the wagon and my back up. I will transport the female into headquarters." This was strange. His vehicle passed me as I approached the scene. I saw no one in the back seat. I assumed the intoxicated female was in the rear seat lying down.

At 30 mph, we proceeded down bumpy Germantown Ave. The 14th District has limited parking, therefore, while Kelly pulled into the service lane on the left side of the building, I parked in the employee parking lot and walked around to assist. By the time, I arrived, Kelly was in the District laughing and beckoning the inside crew to come outside. He opened the trunk of RPC 1419 and there was the intoxicated female. She appeared to be a confused forty year old Black female about 5'4" tall and 110 pounds. She had been stuffed in the trunk of the car and driven thirteen blocks over a very bumpy highway.

I instantly went into attack mode. I wanted this officer to be arrested. I wanted him punished. I do not remember what I yelled, but a Black Police Officer, by the name of Kenny P., grabbed me and pulled me into the Roll Call Room. Kenny was a stocky but strong guy. Holding firmly onto my shirt, he told me to calm down. I told him that I wanted to report this guy to the Captain. This was cruel and disrespectful treatment that he never would have done to a Caucasian prisoner. Kenny told me, "You only got (sic) less than two years on the job. Who are they going to believe if you make a complaint? They will find a way to fire you. Just be calm. These things will work themselves out. Fight another battle." I did calm down but my anger still boiled inside of me.

Proper procedure for intoxicated females was that rather than be kept in the District as was done with men, they all had to be transported to the Police Headquarters' Detention Unit. EPW 502 was directed to come into the 14th District to transport the woman. Both Kenny and I stood silently in the holding area until the EPW arrived twenty minutes later. Once I was satisfied that she would no longer be abused, I went back on patrol. Being watchful over this helpless woman was important to me. There were rumors about a Lieutenant in 4-Squad who occasionally picked up intoxicated black females and sexually assaulted them. I did not want this to happen to this woman. I do not recall that this woman made a complaint about the way she was transported. Officer Kelly had only a few years to laugh about this incident. He suffered a serious injury several years later that resulted in his dying at a relatively young age.

Outstanding incident number 2 occurred during my second year. A veteran respected African American Police Officer in my squad, Officer Coles, was selected for reassignment to the Captain's undercover vice squad. This seemed like a choice assignment. Most Officers stay in this squad until the Captain's assignment to the district ends. After three weeks, Officer Coles was back in uniform. He told those of us who were close to him that he was dismissed from the unit because he would not accept illegal payments from established vice offenders. These were people who maintained illegal lottery houses or illegal liquor sales houses. I was shocked that this type of systematic corruption occurred. This meant that not only were the Officers involved in corrupt activity, but also the District Commander. After this, I never wanted to have any involvement with vice characters. If per chance I encountered one of them in the normal course of my duties, I would take the proper action. Otherwise, I was not going to actively seek out these people because I did not want to deal with the repercussions, i.e. intervention by other Police Officers. I enjoyed my job and did not want to soil my career by any hint that I interacted with these criminals and the Officers who protected them. A few years later, I would be forced to think otherwise.

Outstanding incident # 3 occurred in autumn of 1968. There was a large gang fight outside of Germantown High School at dismissal time. The school was located a block away from the Police Station. As a large throng of students spilled out onto Germantown Ave., several Police Officers responded. I was not there. Several African American Officers gave me the same account. The majority of the Officers who responded to the near riot were Caucasian Police Officers. Rather than seeking out the core offenders, these Officers "made clubs trump". That was police terminology for meting out justice with their batons and black jacks.

The officers began clubbing students randomly. Those who were clubbed were arrested and charged with assault and disorderly conduct. It was a horrific event. The Police Internal Affairs Unit received several complaints about the incident. The unit began to interview all students arrested and any witnesses they could find. Of course, there were no "police witnesses". At some point, a left wing "do-gooder" group headquartered in the Chestnut Hill Section of the 14th District decided to get involved. They hated Police Officers and often followed Police Vehicles while they were on patrol. We African American Officers discussed this incident among ourselves. Many of the injuries suffered by these students were serious. Many suffered head injuries that required stitches. As we discussed this among ourselves, certain Officers who were known to be brutal were pointed out as offenders in this incident. They were the arresting Officers. These Officers were the targets of an Internal Affairs Bureau investigation.

Because this was a major investigation by Internal Affairs, we felt these Officers would get their just rewards. They needed to be fired and arrested.

We had to stand by silently. None of the police witnesses wanted to come forward to say exactly what happened. That could be a career ending move, especially if no other officers came forward in support. We trusted the system. As the time for the Preliminary Hearing drew near, there were strong rumors that there was sufficient evidence against the arresting officers for them to be subject to disciplinary action up to and including dismissal and arrest. These types of rumors usually had some basis in fact. The arresting Officers seemed very, very nervous. This was odd behavior for an Officer about to appear at a Preliminary Hearing.

At the Preliminary Hearing the District Attorney only had to establish a "prima facie" case against the defendants. That meant showing that a crime had been committed and there was some evidence that the defendants committed the crime. Usually only minimal evidence was submitted. What happened at this hearing was a travesty of justice. The activist group encouraged the defendants to enhance their stories at the hearing. Their enhancements were contradictory to sworn and signed statements they have given to the Police Internal Affairs Bureau and to the District Attorney. Because of the newly sworn statements at the hearing, the Internal Affairs Bureau dismissed the complaints against the Officers. Contradictory sworn statements were sufficient to "unfound" the complaints against the Officers. This angered many of the African American Officers. If the "do-gooders" had stayed out of the investigation, these Officers would have been fired. The charges against the injured defendants were dismissed, later. It was as if the incident never happened.

In September of 1969, I was assaulted by a group of ten juveniles and young men as I attempted to make an arrest in East Germantown in the Unit Block of East Ashmead Street. Ten young adults and juveniles were gambling in an alley between Collum St. and Ashmead St. This location and the gambling activity was a neighborhood nuisance that had been reported to the Police Commissioner. Police Officers observing illegal activity at this location were instructed to give the perpetrators stern warnings and to make arrests when required.

At approximately 9:30pm, I received a radioed assignment to disperse a crowd that was gambling in the alley in the rear of 20 E. Ashmead Street. I walked into the alley. At a "T" intersection in the alley under a lamp post I observed ten males loudly participating in a dice game. I approached the group. They did not move. I decided that due to repeated calls to this location for the same activity that an arrest was warranted. I notified the ten young men, who ranged in age from sixteen to eighteen years of age that I was placing them under arrest. I directed all to my Radio Patrol Car (RPC) which was parked on Ashmead Street. As they walked toward my car, a few began to yell to their friends on Collum Street at the other end of the alley. "Hey, we got a pussy in the alley trying to lock us up", one of them yelled.

At this point, members of the Brickyard Gang attempted to interfere with the arrests. I was alone. In addition to physically fighting with the group, I was pelted with glass, rocks, and other debris. As I battled to hold on to my weapon and a prisoner, I shot two of the offenders. Neither was seriously wounded. It took several minutes before I was able to grab my police radio and ask for assistance. Remember, in those days, Police Officers in vehicles did not have portable radios. Fortunately, a civilian called from a telephone to alert the Police Department that an Officer was in need of help. This was a learning opportunity. Everyone doesn't respect or obey Police Officers. There are bad people in the world who look for opportunities to injure Police Officers. Ten offenders ranging in age from 16 – 18 years old were arrested. I was blessed. My injuries kept me away from the job for a month. Although I was given an opportunity to transfer to another assignment, I elected to return to the 14th District.

During the 1970's, the Police Department and several Human Interest Groups decided it would be a good idea to institute racial sensitivity training to veteran Police Officers. This training would become a permanent "In Service" training program. It seemed to be a good idea. The training program was held on Temple University's campus. These seminars were brutal. The Instructors were experienced in teaching Human Relations courses at Temple University. A program that should have been beneficial to the Police Department turned out to be a painful exhibition of poor behavior by many Police Officers.

Of particular concern was the behavior of Officers who worked in the Northeast and Eastern Police Districts. The Northeast Police Division was populated predominantly by middle to upper middle class Caucasian families. The Eastern Police Districts were in the midst of change from predominantly blue-collar working class Caucasians to Hispanic and

African Americans in certain portions. Many of the Officers in these classes persisted in interrupting the Instructors and berated them for their lack of "street knowledge". These Officers wore their racist collars on their blue sleeved shirts. They voiced their opinions without fear because there was never any Police Supervision attending these seminars. Supposedly, Police Commanders were monitoring these classes. I never saw this done. I believe this was a purposefully designed protests by Police Management to sabotage these classes.

The Police Officers were free to voice their unnervingly biased opinions. I was always frustrated and embarrassed when I attended these seminars. These seminars were non-productive. Despite the urging of some of us in asking the bigots and disrupters to keep quiet so that we could get out of class early, these self-centered sociopaths in blue could not resist any opportunity to vocalize their ignorance. No civilian was going to teach/ show them how to be sensitive to minorities. All that mattered was they were the blue clothed guardians of ignorance. Their goal was to protect the status quo in their fading bastions of de facto segregation. I often asked myself how these Neanderthals passed the Police Department's Psychological Examination during the pre-hire interview process. By the way, most of the Instructors for this program were African-American. I am sure they had interesting stories to tell their superiors and families about the behaviors of their "students". I wonder if any of these Instructors became members of groups that monitored instances of police misconduct.

These early days of my police career were times of change. The Philadelphia Police Department was engaged in hiring proportionally more non-white Police Officers. This was a direct result of a federal investigation after the riot of 1964. One of the findings of this investigation was that the amount of minority Police Officers in the Philadelphia Police Department was out of proportion with the percentage of non-white citizens in the city. It was felt that a greater presence of African American Police Officers in predominantly African American neighborhoods would lower the possibility of riots in the future. Citizens would be more comfortable relating to people who looked like them. It was a dumb conclusion.

People wanted to be respected by Police Officers, no matter what color they were. What I found in my short career was that many Caucasian Police Officers feared interaction with African-Americans. They viewed African

Americans as an overly sensitive, ignorant war-like people. Obviously, they watched too many Tarzan movies. If an African American male called some Caucasian Officer a "white mother......" that would likely result in an arrest. Conversely, if that same person called an African American Officer a "black, Uncle Tom mother......" the remark would either be ignored or there would be a verbal effort to mollify the hostility. I saw these behaviors repeated many times. I remember that when I was interviewed for employment as a Police Officer, I was asked how I would react to a protester calling me a "nigger" or "Uncle Tom". My answer was that you cannot react to name calling. You have to focus on your mission. There was that old saying about "Stick and stones may break my bones, but names will never hurt me." Name calling does hurt but you weaken the name caller by not responding. Some Police Officers forgot that simple but important advice. Please remember that on both sides of the aforementioned scenarios there were exceptions. To paraphrase an old joke, "Every White Police Officer was not your enemy. Every Black Police Officer was not your friend."

During the time between 1967 and 1970, there were many revolutionary groups with various reasons for hating the government or representatives of the government. Among these groups were the Weather Underground Organization (Weathermen), Students for a Democratic Society, The Revolutionary Youth Movement, and the Black Panther Party. These groups considered themselves at war with the United States Government. They frequently threatened and killed Police Officers. Because these groups had many sympathizers, most of whom were non-violent, Police Officers developed a "them against us" culture. In addition, if, as a Police Officer, you complained about any bad behavior of a Police Officer, you were looked upon as a "fink", or a "traitor". You, immediately, were ostracized because you were a part of "them" and not "us". The Fraternal Order of Police, Lodge 5 was/is the bargaining agent for most Philadelphia Police Officers. It was at one of their weekly meetings that I first heard the words, ".....we are all blue. There is no Black, no White, and no Yellow. We are all blue." During my career this phrase was repeated over and over, particularly when certain organizations such as The Guardian Civic League (which I will speak of later), and the National Association for the Advancement of Colored People (NAACP) complained about the disparity in the treatment of African American Officers and African American citizens by the Philadelphia Police Department. When the FOP felt under threat, the mantra was "we are all blue". In practice, race mattered.

During the period between 1967 and 1970, five Philadelphia Police Officers were murdered due to hostile encounters with criminals. The most glaring of these was the assassination of Sergeant Frank R. Von Colin. Sergeant Von Colin was part of a unit known as the Park Police or Park Guards. Their patrol duties were restricted to Philadelphia's expansive Fairmount Park. In 1972, this group was incorporated into the Philadelphia Police Department. On Saturday, August 29, 1970, while sitting in his office, Sergeant Von Colin was assassinated by a group calling themselves "The Revolutionaries". These Black urban terrorists, also, seriously wounded several Police Officers after the assassination of Sgt. Von Colin. These deadly assaults became the catalyst for the "them or us" mentality.

Even back in 1968, when I observed that intoxicated woman transported in the trunk of a police car, my protestations to anyone in authority would not only have fallen on deaf ears, but would have likely resulted in the termination of my police career. Police Officers passionately hate other Police Officers who expose the bad behavior of other Police Officers. Still, I knew that I could do certain things on my own without causing a big fuss. Everyone knew that I could not be "paid off" by criminals. Everyone knew that I disdained brutalizing prisoners. Once the resistance stopped, we should stop. We were professionals, not thugs. Eventually, some Police Officers behaved differently around me. They were always afraid that I would not be one to support them if they did something wrong. I might "fink them out." In my own little way, I was making a difference.

Whenever I had a partner, that partner was a new or "rookie" Officer. Those Officers never learned from me about where to "pick up a note". They did experience how to talk to people without inflaming a situation. You had to learn how to be flexible. Every person who commits a traffic violation does not deserve a summons. Try to build a bridge rather than create a chasm. There were times when I drove a bit too fast. Several accidents later, I learned to follow the safety reminders, "On an emergency call, time is of the essence, but no time is lost that is used for safety. An emergency is no excuse for an accident." Part of my zeal to get to the scene of a possible crime was my observance of how lackadaisical many of my co-workers were in their response to emergency situations. I, clearly, remember working with a veteran Officer who when we received an assignment of "Robbery in Progress, Man with a Gun", opted to go the Doughnut Shop at Germantown and Chelten Aves. rather than acknowledge the assignment. You cannot imagine how frustrating this was. By the end of 1968, I considered myself a fully trained Police Officer. I was trusted to train new Officers. I was totally indoctrinated with police terminology. It was mostly negative terminology. People outside of the department are either "cop lovers" or "jerkoffs/assholes". Lawyers were "bottom feeders". We called sneakers, "felony shoes" because most criminals fleeing crime scenes wore sneakers. In those days, most people were still wearing shoes rather than sneakers.

By November 1968, I made my first appearance in a Philadelphia newspaper. I was cited as having been involved in the first felony arrest using the newly issued portable police radios. I was able to broadcast the description of a robbery suspect who committed a robbery of an ice cream parlor at Wayne Ave. and Queen Lane. Prior to the announcement of the robbery, the perpetrator ran past me and into the housing project at 301 Queen Lane, which was two blocks away. Two months earlier, prior to the issuance of these radios, this criminal would not have been caught. We were able to apprehend him in thirty minutes. Although there was mention of this arrest in the newspaper, there were no accolades from the Police Department. It would be a while before I learned that outspoken Officers do not easily earn commendations. By the end of 1968, I had seen a drunken woman abused; learned that even Police Commanders could be corrupt; and learned that exposing these miscarriages of justice would only serve to arouse the scum who wanted end my chosen career. I had to be the captain of my own ship, on my own sector, in my own car. I had to treat people the best that I could whenever I could and never tolerate others abusing their authority while I was present.

By the end of 1968, five Police Officers, including two whom I knew, were killed in the line of duty. One of the most disturbing was the "negligent homicide" of a Police Officer in our district. Two partners worked in the 14th District but not in my squad. Both were permanently assigned to an Emergency Patrol Wagon. They were known to get along well together. Both were extremely playful. One particular evening, they had to drive their Emergency Patrol Wagon to the 35th Police District for lubrication and oil service. While this service was being done on their vehicle, the two decided to play a game of "Quick Draw". These were veteran Police Officers. In their game, one was to match his speed at drawing a knife while his partner was drawing a gun. This was similar to a scene in the movie the Magnificent Seven featuring James Coburn as the knife welder. Unfortunately, a gun accidentally discharged in this exercise of stupidity. One Officer died. After an investigation, the offending Officer's employment was terminated and he was criminally charged with negligent homicide. While the death of any Officer in the line of duty is tragic, the end results of this killing was puzzling. In 1971, former Police Commissioner Frank L. Rizzo was campaigning for Mayor of Philadelphia. During one of his campaign stops, I saw the offending Officer operating a sound truck for Mr. Rizzo. Ironically, the truck was driving through Chelten Ave., in the 14th Police District. This was this disgraced Officer's former district of assignment. I found it strange that a former Police Commissioner would employ someone who had killed another Police Officer. I mentioned this to several Officers, but I was met with a collective shrug. Frank L. Rizzo was a person who was viewed no lower than the Second Coming of the Messiah by many Police Officers. He was a boorish, right-wing brute whose leadership qualities could be viewed as fascist rather than democratic. While he embraced his sycophants, he tried to destroy his critics. Months after Rizzo was elected mayor, I had to appear in court for a criminal trial. I was shocked to see the offending former Police Officer dressed in a Sheriff's uniform and escorting prisoners into the courtroom. Was this cronyism to the extreme? I was looking at a disgraced former Police Officer wearing a badge of authority. I was speechless. This was not the end of this story.

A few years later, after Frank L. Rizzo had won re-election as Mayor, I would see just how ridiculous fascist cronyism can be. I had to check in for a scheduled court appearance with the Court Attendance Unit at City Hall. As I was standing in line waiting to check in, guess who was in line in front of me? That disgraced former Officer was fully outfitted as a Police Officer. He was checking in for a Court Appearance. Fortunately, I am not one prone to fainting. The Court Attendance Clerks were all

Police Officers. I checked in with an Officer with whom I had worked some years previous. In whispered tone, I asked, "Do you know who that was? " The Officer replied with a whispered tone of disgust, "Yeah, he's in the 26th District."

Wow!! How could this happen? How could you kill another Police Officer either purposely or negligently, and find yourself re-employed as a Police Officer. This was outrageous. It was never reported in the news media. Everyone from the Police Commissioner to the Personnel Clerk kept quiet about this. There was no leak to the media. This demonstrated the almost Orwellian authority of Frank L. Rizzo. If not respected, he was a man who had to be feared.

By the end of 1970, I learned that fear and ostracization are the maintenance tools for encapsulating the "Code of Silence" or "Blue Wall" that is known to the public. I, always called it the "Code of Omerta". This is the same code enforced by the Mafia and other criminal organizations. Anytime you actively use fear and coercion to grind the wheels of truth and justice to a halt, you are no longer a law enforcement Officer. You are a criminal. This was never discussed at the Police Academy or at any training I received during my first 23 years on the Police Department. This is why you can have a Police Officer whose squad was nearly disbanded because of rampant corruption employed as an Instructor for Vice Crimes at the Police Academy in 1967. This was the mixed message the Police Department sent to all Police Recruits and Police Veterans. What was the demarcation line between cops and crooks? Though vaguely defined by policies, it was ill-defined in practice. One could be removed from the Vice Squad for not accepting illegal payments from criminals to ignore their behavior. One could kill a fellow Officer and still be employed as a Police Officer. Was I working for a Law Enforcement Agency or was I working for a criminal organization? The fence cannot be straddled. One dirty foot corrupts the entire body. By the end of 1971, I learned that The Police Department's crime eradication strategy was best accomplished with an eraser and a lack of compassionate leadership. What a milieu! This practice had a direct negative impact on middle-class and impoverished neighborhoods. A lower crime rate justifies employing fewer Police Officers. The Fraternal Order of Police never caught on to this. What kind of bargaining agent did I have?

Moving On

By the February 1971, my career had experienced the death of eleven Police Officers. All died in the line of duty. Some died fighting crime. Some were purposely assassinated. Police ranks drew closer together. The "us versus them" mentality permeated the department. I still struggled with working among some of the laziest and irresponsible Police Officers. There were some pitiful cases.

One Officer came to work intoxicated almost every day. He had to work an Emergency Patrol Wagon with a partner. While this may seem outrageous to many, we took it as being charitable. In 1968, he was one of several Officers who responded to a "Robbery in Progress" alarm at a Germantown supermarket. So many of these alarms are accidentally tripped. This was not one of them. One of the first Officers to respond walked into the supermarket and was immediately shot in the thigh before he could react. This second Officer encountered two males exiting the supermarket with guns drawn. As this Officer drew his pistol, he warned the men to stop and to drop their weapons. They did not. The nearest male fired his gun. The bullet missed the Officer. The Officer fired his weapon and struck the offender with five bullets. The male walked several steps toward the Officer before finally collapsing in front of him. The offender behind him dropped his weapon and surrendered.

That would have been enough of a shock, but there was one additional surprise for this Officer. A swarm of other Officers arrived. One observant Officer noticed a suspicious male sitting in a car near the supermarket. He was parked behind the second Officer to respond. When this male in the car was investigated, Police Officers found that he was a part of the robbery team. He was driving the "getaway car". On the seat next to him was a sawed-off shot gun. When the Officers unloaded the weapon, they found that the shotgun's firing pin had struck the cartridge in the chamber, but the shell misfired. Once that second Officer found out this information, he was never the same. He spent several additional years in the Police Department. He always worked with a partner in the quieter section of a Police District. He was hidden this way because there was no other suitable assignment for him. At that point, there was no provision for the department to deal with post-traumatic stress. There was no psychological treatment program. Because of his bravery, Police Commissioner/Mayor Frank Rizzo determined that he was going to take care of this Officer. He was deemed a minimal risk to the public. He had only a few years to go before retirement.

In the 14th District, we, also, had another Officer who obviously was not mentally fit to be a Police Officer. He often laughed at things that were not funny. There was nothing about the job that he viewed seriously. His problem solving skills were severely deficient. All of us wondered how this guy not only became a Police Officer, but also, how he remained a Police Officer. The prevailing rumor was that his family had a strong political connection to the Police Department and no one should take any action against him. By 1974, his behavior had become so bizarre that he was sent for a mental evaluation.

Despite Police Department warnings not to do this, he would board subway trains in full uniform and give out religious pamphlets to riders. An examination by a Psychiatrist contracted by the City of Philadelphia initially found no abnormalities. Still the bizarre behavior persisted and the Police Department determined that he was a danger to himself and the community. He was committed to a psychiatric hospital. While there, he committed suicide. This was a sad story that could have been much worse if he had been allowed to continue to walk the streets of Philadelphia with a badge and a gun.

By 1971, I had been involved in several vehicle accidents. Not all were my fault, but once one shows a proclivity to get involved in accidents, the department was obliged to take action. I was transferred to the Subway Unit. I appreciated my time in the 14th Police District. There were many memorable milestones. One milestone was the breakup of my first marriage.

Broken marriages were an occupational hazard in the career of a Police Officer. I had been warned.

The Subway Unit's job was to insure public safety on the subway and elevated rail systems in the city. There was no driving involved. I felt it was boring work. After a few months, I applied for an opening in the Police Communication Department (Radio Room). My supervisors felt that I would never get the job because I had no connections. What they did not know as that I was proficient in speaking Spanish. There was a need for bilingual dispatchers. I was accepted, and after about six months in the Subway Unit, I became a Police Communications Dispatcher. I loved that job.

The Police Communications Unit was composed of both civilians and Police Officers. Among the permanent staff were some of the most dedicated professionals I had ever encountered in the Police Department. Everything was "hands on". There were no computers. There were separate consoles for each Police Division and two consoles that served in a citywide capacity for special units and emergencies. Each console was staffed with four to six persons. Each console had a supervisor. Within a year, I was able to move from working at divisional consoles to "J & H" band which was the main communications console for all Police Commanders. A few months after being placed on that console, I received a Commendatory Letter from the Police Commissioner because of the way I handled communications during the pursuit of a robbery suspect in Center City. I learned a lot about how the department functioned internally. This was an invaluable learning tool for me. This wonderful experience began to unravel for me in 1976.

Shortly after he won his re-election to Mayor in 1975, Mayor Rizzo successfully lobbied to have the city wage tax increased by one percent to 4.31%. This tax covers all persons who either live in or work within the city of Philadelphia. This was a highly controversial endeavor as his mayoral campaign was marked by his promise not to raise taxes. Taxes were always rising, so this was not a big concern for me. My concern, although small, should have had a simple answer. None was forthcoming. The effective date of the tax increase was July 1st. We received a pay the following week. This pay was for the last two weeks in June. My concern was, if we earned pay under the old wage tax, why was that pay subject to the new tax increase? Again, it seemed like a simple question but all I wanted was an answer.

No one within my work sphere could give me an answer. True to my military training, I went up the "Chain of Command". On a Departmental Memorandum Form, I sent this request through channels to Police Commissioner Joseph F. O'Neil. I waited a few days. I did not receive a reply. Somewhere along the chain of progression, some commander should have seen the memorandum and should have been able to send me a reply. "None of your business" would have sufficed, but I should have received a reply. I called the Fraternal Order of Police. The representative seemed flustered by the question. "I will ask around and get back to you", he stated. I waited a few days. No one called me back. Next, I sent the same letter to the Mayor Frank L. Rizzo, City Controller William Klenk, and City Finance Director Lennox Moak. Truly frustrated, I vented my ire by sending the same question to the Philadelphia Daily News. There was silence from everyone.

About a week later, because of my duties as Treasurer for the Guardian Civic League, I was invited to a dinner where several politicians and civic leaders were in attendance. The Guardian Civic League is an organization predominantly comprised of African American Police Officers of all ranks. It serves as a conduit for all concerns of the African American community or African American Police Officers about inequities experienced from the Philadelphia Police Department. While at this dinner, I was fortunate enough to meet City Controller William Klenk. He was one of the city officials to whom I had sent my concern. He was very personable and quite approachable. During the "meet and greet" portion of the dinner (cocktail hour), I took the bold chance to introduce myself to him. When I related to him my letter of concern, he immediately replied that he had read it and had brought it to the attention of City Finance Director Lennox Moak. Mr. Klenk stated that the Finance Director controls all tax related issues. Mr. Moak had told him that he sets the start date of any tax increase and no one, except the Mayor (who appointed him), can rescind that. We both shrugged our shoulders. I was not overjoyed with the answer, but it was an answer. I was willing to accept it and I mentally tabled the matter.

About a week later, while working the 3pm – 11pm shift, I was sitting at my console in the Radio Room when one of my co-workers told me that he had read my editorial in the Philadelphia Daily News. I was shocked. I had no idea the letter would be printed. In fact, it had been almost three weeks since I had sent the letter. Within minutes, it seemed as though everyone in the Communications Unit was talking about the editorial. I told those who were near me that I had spoken to Controller Klenk and that he gave me a satisfactory answer. I had totally forgotten about the issue. My console was near one of the exit doors of the Radio Room. I happened to notice Police Commissioner O'Neill enter the Inspector's Office and leave a few minutes later. About twenty minutes later, my squad Lieutenant told me that the Inspector wanted to talk to me in his office. Up until that moment, I had never seen the Inspector.

The Inspector had a very small office. I stood at "parade rest" in front of him as he sat at his desk. He told me that the Police Commissioner was very concerned about my editorial. He asked if I had asked anyone for permission to write the editorial. I related to him that I had sent my question through channels and had also contacted the Fraternal Order of Police. I told him that no one responded to me. I, also, told him that I had spoken to City Controller Klenk and that he gave me an answer to my question over a week ago. The Inspector told me that in the future, I should ask for permission before submitting editorials concerning the Police Department or the city to newspapers. He asked me to promise that I would never again send an editorial concerning Police practices to a newspaper. I was shocked. I was also, shocked by my quick response. "I can't promise you that, sir." "Why", he responded. "Sir, I have a constitutional right to voice my opinion. I cannot promise you that I will never do that." Sternly, he looked at me and verbatim repeated his directive. My reply was the same. Verbatim he repeated his directive a third time. A light went off in my head. He was told to tell me this by the Police Commissioner. The Commissioner wanted a specific response. Without that response, this trapped Inspector was not going to let me out of his office. "Sir, if I decide to write another editorial concerning the city or the Police Department, I will be sure to submit it for approval." Immediately, thereafter, he gave me permission to return to work. I thought that would be the end of it. Three weeks later, I was transferred to the 5th Police District. I was distraught. Was this retaliation?

"God's Country" - The 5th Police District

(Camaraderie is a great thing until you use it as a weapon.)

One of my co-workers in the Radio Room tried to console me by telling me that being transferred to the 5th District was nothing to get upset about. The Police Department was trying to "teach me a lesson" without really hurting me. The 5th District was considered "God's Country". There were never that many calls for Police Service. It was a "retirement home." Why did I need a "retirement home"? I had just a little more than ten years on the job. I was still too full of energy to want to sit in a police car contemplating what I was going to do after retiring. Little did I know that working in the 5th Police District would require acumen gleaned from my North Philly upbringing, my military career, my education, my knowledge of proper police procedures, and most of all my integrity.

The socialization and systemization of evil is a process as subtle as the serpent in the Garden of Eden. In law enforcement, once the evil seed is sown, it is fertilized by the guile of the opportunist and the hand-shaded eyes of the meek. Once this garden is watered by public indifference, it will grow faster than mold in a dark moist closet. Once you are in the stench long enough, you become almost immune to its sickening smell. It was during my tenure in the 5th Police District, that I created the phrase, "People under water don't feel wet."

A few years prior to coming to the 5th Police District, while sitting in a Barber's chair at 18th & Wingohocking Street, I heard a customer pose this question about Police Officers taking money to ignore illegal activities; "What's the problem, they're all doing it?" The Barber had no problem cutting the hair on the back of my neck. It was standing erect. My blood boiled. I was a "cop". I would never ever take money to ignore illegal activity. I had to make sure that throughout my career I would never be painted with the same scummy brush as those crooks with badges.

The 5th District Saga Begins

As I began to dust off some of my police gear, I was full of wonder about tackling my new assignment. Surely, I would not be treated the same way I had been treated in my rookie days in the 14th District, which shared a portion of its border with the 5th District. I was a ten-year veteran. I would likely be allowed to work alone at the very beginning. Such was not the case. One must be oriented to whatever their new district assignment might be. There were a few purposes for this. Verbally, you were told that you required a few days to become acquainted with the geography of the district. The second reason was more important. Once you were transferred to a different district assignment, someone in the receiving district has already called someone in your former district or former assignment to find out what type of person you are. "Is he a jerkoff?" "Can he be trusted?" "Is he a rat"? Those are the primary questions asked. Within hours of this conversation, a misty rendering of your personality has been broadcasted, via the rumor mill, to all members of the receiving district. The first few days of your reassignment, you are working with Officers who are noting every nuance of your personality so that they can give a "true" rendering of you to the Sergeant and other Officers. That is really not a bad thing. Everyone needs to know if you can be relied upon in an emergency situation. Are you a hot head? In a hostile confrontation are you more likely to take a step backward or take a step forward. These are important and necessary characteristics other Officers must know so that they can gauge your reliability.

My journey in the 5th Police District began in September, 1976. Sergeant Parker (not his real name) was my Platoon Sergeant. He was a friendly and serious supervisor. All of my squad members seemed to be friendly dedicated professionals. Lieutenant Clemens (not his real name) was my Squad Commander. Captain Herschel Simpson (not his real name) was my District Commander. I was ready to settle in and get acquainted with my new assignment. My first two or three weeks, I worked in varied sections of the district with an assortment of partners. Within a month, I could find most streets in this sprawling district on the Northwestern terminus of the city without using my Street Guide. There was no GPS during these days. You had to read the Street Guide or refer to a map to get around. Fortunately, the normal workload in this district allowed you more than enough time to familiarize yourself with streets and passageways that would be difficult to find on a map. People unfamiliar with the district would have a difficult time locating an intersection such as "Minerva & Bean Streets" with or without a map. Unlike many districts, the 5th Police District was an extremely hilly area. It was comprised of the communities of Wissahickon, Manayunk, Roxborough, and Andorra. You could not drive safely in this area if you had not developed the skill of parking your vehicle on a hill. Extremely good judgement was required to parallel park in many areas. On approximately October 12, 1976, Sgt. Parker told me that because of an Officer's recent transfer, Radio Patrol Car 57 would be my steady car.

Radio Patrol Car 57's sector was bordered by Shurs Lane on the south end; Levering Street on the north end; Terrace Street on the east end; and the Manayunk Canal on the west end. Main Street, which runs parallel to and is adjacent to the Manayunk Canal contains the majority of the businesses in the sector. The highest concentration of businesses were in the 4200 and 4300 blocks of Main Street or between Roxborough Ave. and Levering St. It was a blue collar, working class neighborhood. There was a small concentration of African Americans in the area. There did not appear to be any hint of animosity between the races. Yes, this was an ideal neighborhood for a steady assignment. Small shops in a close knit area. This seemed far different than my steady sectors many years ago in the 14th Police District. I could handle this.

One of the more popular spots in the district was a restaurant that looked like a typical greasy spoon eatery. It was open twenty-four hours. It featured both eat-in and take-out food. Several of the Officers I worked with during my orientation went there to get sandwiches. Of course, I went there with them. This place was popular because the owner authorized free sandwiches and a beverage to Officers who worked in the area. I was never comfortable patronizing establishments that gave food or other items away. I avoided them.

Across the street from the restaurant were a bicycle shop, a pawn shop, scuba diving gear shop, and Rose's Drug Store. During normal business hours, this area was quite busy. Typical of the majority of "main streets" in Philadelphia, there was parking on both sides of the street and there was one driving lane in each direction. One evening Sergeant Parker met with me to sign my patrol log. This was normal procedure. He asked me if I was having any problems with my new assignment. I told him that everything seemed to be fine. I was not having any problems. Just prior to his driving away, he told me to try to avoid having anything to do with the popular restaurant and its proprietor Rocco "Rocky" Barba. He said that he knew several Officers went in there but his personal preference was to stay away. I took this as a warning to be heeded.

One good thing about an area such as this, was that you had an opportunity to introduce yourself to the business people and some of the residents. Almost all of the business people on Main St. were friendly. Many were quick to engage in conversations when customers were not around. This was a great way to learn of their concerns.

On the day and evening shifts, I often put myself out of service for security checks in the 4300 block of Main St. I could park my police vehicle and walk into several stores. I knew the merchants took comfort in this and I began to form a close relationship with many of them. There was one consistent theme to many of their conversations. Most voiced their mistrust of "Rocky". They were particularly upset about an old blue Chevrolet that "Rocky" kept parked illegally in a bus stop in front of his store. "Rocky" used this old vehicle to store trash and garbage from his restaurant. This was his private, illegally parked dumpster. The vehicle was parked in a Bus Stop for the Route 61 SEPTA bus.

On trash collection days, city Trash Collectors knew to go directly to this car to pick up the trash and garbage. This was a health hazard and an eyesore. I vowed to deal with this situation. The problem existed long before my arrival to the 5th District. I consulted with other Officers. Their collective response was that everyone ignored the vehicle because

"Rocky loves a cop" and he gave out free food to Officers. My suspicion was confirmed. This was a quid pro quo relationship. Despite this vehicle presenting a health and driving hazard, Police Officers chose to ignore it. Obtaining a free meal was more important to them. I had an immediate memory flashback to an incident in the 14th Police District.

The Toddle House Restaurant was located in the center of the main business district on Wayne Ave., north of Chelten Ave. The business was located in front of a bus stop for the Route K SEPTA bus. Because this location was on my sector of responsibility, I frequently warned customers to move their cars. When I could not locate the owner, I would issue a parking summons. The Toddle House was frequented by several Officers. My dealings with the restaurant became solely of a business nature after I learned that this was the meeting place for a group of burglars headed by a guy known as "Little Nicky."

One summer evening, circa 7:30pm, I noticed a vehicle parked in front of the restaurant in the center of the bus stop. This was an extremely hazardous condition because the large passenger bus was exiting a left turn from westbound Chelten Ave. When the bus made that left turn, parked vehicles made the turn hazardous to riders and pedestrians about to board the bus. I went into the restaurant and politely asked if the vehicle belonged to anyone. The restaurant was crowded. I had to ask loudly twice. No one responded. The nearby waitress shrugged her shoulders. I left the restaurant and began to write out a parking violation summons. Once, I began write the summons, a small group of men and women ran out of the restaurant and approached me. The woman who led the crowd, asked me why I was writing a summons. I told her that the vehicle was illegally parked in the bus stop. Someone yelled, "Hey, we always park here. Nobody bothers us. This car's not hurting anybody." Directing my voice to the male, I told him that this was an illegal parking zone, and I was enforcing the regulation. The female became irate. The crowd became verbally hostile. Just to set the scene, this entire crowd was composed of Caucasian men and women. I held no racial animosity towards them. I was just trying to get the car moved. Because of the growing hostility, I asked for another car to back me up. Police Officer Kenny P., in RPC 145 arrived. The woman became more obstinate. She opened the door of her vehicle and sat in it. I completed writing the summons. The crowd had swollen to about twenty men and women. They continued to loudly voice their protest. I placed the summons on the windshield of the car. I tapped on her closed window and told her that she would have to move the car or I would have it towed away. She yelled through the closed window that she as not moving the car. Now, people began to gather from outside of the supermarket across the street. I knew that many of the group supporting this woman were part of the burglary ring. I had arrested one of them, Fred P., a few months earlier.

I told the woman that if she did not move the vehicle immediately, I was going to arrest her for disorderly conduct and have her vehicle towed. She remained defiant. I called for an Emergency Patrol Wagon (EPW) to transport her to the Police District. Because this was a popular location, several police vehicles responded along with the EPW. My thinking was that on seeing the EPW, the woman would calm down and be reasonable. Edged on by her cronies, she became more defiant. I told her that she was under arrest and that I would forcibly enter the vehicle to make that arrest. "Fuck you, I'm not moving", was her response. "Leave her alone", was voiced by the crowd. Except for Kenny, all of the arriving Police Officers stood far away from me. They appeared to be in shock. Normally, someone would come over to ask for an assessment. One Officer on the EPW crew yelled, "Why don't you just give her the ticket and leave?" I yelled back at

*him, "She's under arrest and you are taking her." I think the
officers were worried about their free sandwiches.*

*I pulled out my compressed paper baton and gave one hard
pound to the driver's side window. There was a large gasp.
I was known as a low-keyed, soft spoken person. All of the
Police Officers were in shock. The male with the loudest voice,
Mr. Big Mouth, ran over to the car. He told the woman to
get out of the car and to go with me. "We will follow you to
the Police Station." The woman obeyed. Proper procedure
was for all prisoners to be handcuffed. The wagon crew was
hesitant to do this. I placed my own handcuffs on the woman.
This was a safety issue. The EPW transported her to the
district. Once inside of the Police Station, she was a bit
calmer. I obtained her identification and began to prepare
the paperwork for a disorderly conduct summons.*

*As I was preparing the paperwork, it seemed as though the
entire restaurant crowd came storming through the front door
of the station. Mr. Big Mouth asked to speak to a Supervisor.
Corporal Smeckler (not his real name) went to the window.
Mr. Big Mouth asked if he could speak to him outside of the
Operations Room. The Corporal left the room and was out of
my view as I continued to prepare the paperwork. After about
five minutes, the Corporal returned. "Look Carter", he began,
"These are good people. Just write up a '48 (abbreviation for
Form 75-48, an Incident Report) and say that you brought
her into the district and released her with a warning." I was
steamed. Still, I was a young Officer and he was a Supervisor.
I complied. On this level, the Corporal or Operations Room
Supervisor, must approve all arrests or citations. I was the
very low man on the totem pole. I was suspicious about the
conversation he had with Mr. Big Mouth. The Corporal
never gave me the courtesy of relating the substance of his
discussion with Mr. Big Mouth.*

Now, I go back to the 5th Police District and the business community. Further south on Main St. was a popular night club. It was owned by two prominent, but retired, National Football League players. As with all properties, I checked this premises on all shifts. One afternoon, while making a security check, I had a chance to meet one of the owners. I introduced myself and told him that I was newly assigned to RPC 57. He was very friendly. He grew up in the "Pulaski Town" section of Germantown. My second wife grew up with his entire family. They attended the same church. Both owners were friendly. They asked if I could check inside once or twice every evening when I worked the evening shifts. This was not a problem. It, also, was not an unusual request from an owner of a large restaurant or night club. The key was to be seen but not be intrusive. About two weeks after this first meeting, both owners met me as I was making an afternoon security check of the building. They were sitting outside as workers were preparing for the evening's customers. They were very somber. Both were upset and concerned because the district's "5 Squad Officers" had approached them that day and asked for a contribution to buy uniforms for the 5th District's Police Officers who played on the district's baseball teams. They refused to contribute. The "5 Squad Officers" who were supposedly soliciting on behalf of the District Captain, showed they were very displeased with this refusal. They told the owners that this was a way of showing their appreciation for Officers protecting the community. It was as if the owners were paying "protection dues". I found this behavior by the 5 Squad Officers to be very unusual. Throughout my assignments in the 14th Police District and the Police Communications Unit, I always played on my squad's basketball, baseball, and touch football teams. We always chipped in to pay for our shirts. You wore your own pants and sneakers. Sometimes, businesses would contribute and sponsor teams. None was ever coerced. We always played against either different squads in our own district or members of the same squad (because of we had the same days off) in different districts. It was a great way to stay in shape and a good way to establish and to maintain squad morale. The owners viewed the actions of the "5 Squad Officers" as being suspicious. As did I. Why weren't they trying to apprehend burglars, thieves, and other criminals? That was their job. Soliciting funds was not. I decided to keep a watchful eye on the district's 5 Squad Officers.

It was about this same time that by virtue of my activities in the Guardian Civic League, that I was requested to participate in a local television show entitled "Meetinghouse". The program dealt with community interests and was produced on local television station KYW. The emcee of the program was Matt Quinn. The program featured a "town hall" setting in which topics affecting Philadelphia were discussed. The subject matter of this particular program was, "Does Racism Exist in the Philadelphia Police Department?" The Guardian Civic League had been active as an "amicus of the court" in a civil rights suit alleging that the Philadelphia Police Department discriminated in the hiring of Black and non-Caucasian applicants to the Police Department. In addition, after hiring, the Police Department had a quota system for the number of Black Police Officers promoted to supervisory ranks. This program was supposed to be a one hour taping that would appear the following week.

Members of my organization, The Guardian Civic League, were quite vocal in our weekly meetings about the inequitable treatment meted out by the Police Department in hiring, promotion, and in its treatment of the Black citizens of Philadelphia. I was ready for an intense program and I was sure our group of about fifteen Officers would make an informative presentation on this program. Once we arrived at the studio, we found that there were about ten members of the Executive Staff of the Fraternal Order of Police (FOP). All were Caucasian. After about fifteen minutes into the taping, it appeared to me that the only people freely speaking were the Executive Staff of the FOP. They seemed to be presenting an apparent cogent case for their not being racism in the Police Department. It was that "We are all blue" nonsense that I had heard at the weekly FOP meetings. My Guardian Civic League members seemed to be hesitant in countering statements made by the FOP. African American Police Officers speaking out on television was a new and risky endeavor. There was the fear of departmental repercussions. I felt that this was an opportunity for us to speak out about injustices just as we spoke out about them behind our closed doors. This was why I joined the Police Department. I did not want to be a disrupter. I just wanted to make the department better. I was a relatively new member of the Guardian Civic League (GCL) and I was steaming inside.

Once the steam within me seemed to blow through my ears, I raised my hand and began to talk. I was loud. I was passionate. I was factual. I made several statements, which I honestly cannot recall. What I do remember was that I was adamant and forceful in my assertion that racism existed to an uncomfortable degree within the Police Department. The FOP countered my assertions and other members of the GCL began to support my statements. The debate became heated. At the end of one hour, Program Moderator Matt Quinn told us that the program had become so informative and emotional that it would be spread over two one-hour segments in the succeeding weeks.

After the program, Matt Quinn spoke to me personally. He thanked me for being so vocal and bringing certain issues to light. He stated that should I receive any retaliation from the Philadelphia Police Department or the City of Philadelphia that I should contact him and he would expose this behavior. I thanked him. After my appearance on this program I was requested to appear on several television and radio programs to discuss poor police practices as they related to the Black Community.

The day after the Meetinghouse Program aired, I was working the day shift in RPC 57. Every time I tried to communicate via Police Radio, other Officers would key their radio transmitter buttons. This would either completely block my transmission or render my transmission unintelligible. Because of my experience in the Radio Room, I switched to the alternate City-Wide Band, known as "J Band" to make my transmissions. Normally, this should have been done in emergency situations only. I knew this was annoying to the broadcasters on "J Band" because this meant they would have to relay my message to Northwest Band. Eventually, a civilian dispatcher asked me to call him. He wanted to know why my transmissions were being interfered with. I explained that I thought the behavior of these Officers was due to my appearance on Meetinghouse. Interfering with my broadcast was a cowardly and juvenile protest about my appearance on the program and my statements. The behavior of these mental midgets only served to show me that I was correct in my statements. After about a week of this stupid behavior, it abated. I think the reason for this abatement occurred when I switched over to "J-Band", which was used by the top Police Officials. At one point, I said that Officers were purposely interfering with my transmissions. Immediately, after I made that statement, the Dispatcher stated a frequent radio quip over J-Band and

Northwest Band. The quip was similar to "Attention all Police. Anyone found damaging police radio equipment or interfering with Police Radio broadcast is in violation of section _____ of the Police Duty Manual and is subject to immediate dismissal." No one ever told me this, but I suspect that a whispered order was circulated that if the stupid behavior persisted, someone was going to get caught and possibly lose their job. My television appearance would soon be forgotten if they would just stop bringing attention to themselves. This alarming behavior was miniscule in comparison to behavior exhibited in the coming months. Still, I was confident that I had done my part to expose practices that needed to stop. This was my reason for joining the Police Department. My ideals were being tested. If you cannot stand up for your beliefs, you are nothing more than a "sounding brass or a tinkling cymbal."

As with any assignment or environment, I tried to do the best that I could to fit in with my co-workers without having to compromise my values. I enjoyed participating in squad activities such as football and baseball outings. These types of activities were always good for fostering a better understanding of and appreciation of one's co-workers. I began to observe the two members of the Captain's "5 Squad Officers". These were two Police Officers who worked the day shift. Most 5 Squad Officers were either involved in supplemental crime suppression or community outreach programs. This supplemental force under the direct command of the Captain existed in almost every Police District.

Residential burglaries were a large problem within the city. From personal experience, I can assert that few things are as emotionally draining as to return home and find that someone has entered your domicile and taken away items you cherish. It is a crime that lingers in one's consciousness and sub-consciousness for years after the event.

The 5 Squad Officers in the 5th Police District functioned differently than 5 Squad Officers in other districts. In other districts, some 5 Squad Officers patrolled throughout the district attempting to apprehend burglars and other criminals either shortly after the commission of a crime or while the crime was in progress. Supposedly, they studied crime patterns and designed their patrol areas based on those patterns. They were not investigators. Investigations fell under the responsibilities of Detective Divisions. In the 5th District, after a Police Officers responded to a complaint of a burglary from a citizen, he would complete a thorough Incident Report (75-48). This report once turned into the Operations Room should have been coded, then sent to the Northwest Detective Division. Strangely, many of these reports were not forwarded directly to the Northwest Detective Division. They would be given to the 5 Squad Officers for "further investigation", then forwarded to the Northwest Detective Division. The 5 Squad Officers would either call or personally interview the complainants to ascertain if any additional items were taken. There was little attempt made to find the identity of the burglar by either searching for identifying markers such as blood or fingerprints. There was no canvassing of the surrounding residents to find out if anyone had seen suspicious persons either around, entering, or exiting the subject property. I found this very strange. In addition, I frequently saw the 5 Squad Officers using their vehicle to transport Rocco "Rocky" Barba to unknown locations at various times. Their names were Officer Pauli and Officer Sanger (not their real names).

There had been a few burglaries of businesses on my sector and the adjoining sectors. Most of these burglaries occurred during the evening or overnight shift when the businesses were closed. I, always, took seriously any crime committed on my sector. While other Officers may have taken pride in how many moving violations they had written, I took pride in coming to work and finding out that no crimes had been committed on my sector the previous day while I was working. Suppressing crime and making arrests for criminal activity were my personal priorities. When, I interviewed the owners of businesses that had been burglarized, I tried to stay in contact with them. This was my way of letting them know that I was concerned and that I would be vigilant about doing all that I could to prevent a recurrence. One haunting theme seemed to be repeated by several of the business owners. A day or two after some burglaries, they would receive a call from someone stating that they had property that had been removed from their business and they would return it for a price. Oddly, the owners never wanted to make a report about this phone call. They were afraid of retaliation. I tried to get official statements, but one hundred percent of the owners asked me not to report the phone call. I had to respect their fear, but I needed to find out why all were reticent to file an official complaint. It took several months, but I found my answer.

On an autumn day in 1976, I had come in for my first day of the 4 – 12 shift. As always, I picked up my Part One Sheet and my Stolen Auto Sheet. Much to my surprise, I read that the Night Club on Main Street had been burglarized overnight. Several thousands of dollars in furniture and sound equipment were removed. A burglary of this magnitude required several people and lots of stealth. The night club was recessed about twenty yards off of Main Street. I knew the owners well. I frequently checked on them during my shifts and I had established a good rapport with them. This burglary not only saddened me, it embarrassed me. I had done all that I could to insure the safety of this business. Now, during my days off, someone boldly executed a burglary of this business. After Roll Call, I immediately went to that location and spoke to the owners. They were distraught. They were frustrated. After showing me the damage and stating the extent of the thievery, one of them began to vent his anger. He was adamant in his belief that the "police" had something to do with the burglary. He reminded me of the time when the 5 Squad Officers asked him for money for "baseball team" uniforms. He had refused to make a donation and he felt this was retaliation. I told him that I would do all that I could to find information about the burglary. My investigation led me into the deep and dark waters of malfeasance and suppression.

I contacted three informants in the Manayunk area. These were people whom I had learned to trust. Some were part of the business community. Others were concerned residents. They trusted me. Putting together their information, I was able to accumulate the following scenario for the burglary of the night club.

According to my informants, at least one Police Officer was involved with the night club burglary. Once the Police Officer verified that the owners had closed and left the night club he notified an unknown person. This occurred after 3:00am. That person, notified his team of burglars. They drove a truck to the night club. Police Officer James (not his real name) parked his Radio Patrol Car at the street entrance of the driveway that led to the night club. He remained there until a truck used in the burglary had been loaded. The truck drove to an abandoned store in the 4300 block of Main Street that was owned by "Rocky". The truck backed up to the property's door. This caused the truck to be partially on the sidewalk and partially block Main Street. As items were being taken off the truck and placed into the abandoned store, Police Officer James used his patrol car to block traffic on Main Street at Levering St. This was a very brazen operation that took place at a time when both vehicle and pedestrian traffic were almost non-existent. None of my informants were willing to provide a witness statement to the Detective Division. Thus, my hands were tied. I could do nothing but watch to see if items were being moved out of the store. Nothing occurred on my shifts. I could not share this information with the night club owners. I knew that I could not trust any Police Supervisor or Detective with this information. I had no idea that Police Officers would sink this low in not only aiding but also openly participating in a burglary operation. This salacious saga of systemic complicity would continue.

All parking and moving vehicle summons were obtained from a "ticket book" that each Police Officer must sign for upon receiving it. Each summons had a unique number. This was how the Police Department maintained quality control. One day, I wrote and placed a parking violation summons on Rocco Barba's vehicle that was illegally parked in front of his restaurant. Later that afternoon, I saw Police Officer Sanger of the 5 Squad Officers remove the summons from the vehicle. This was highly unusual. About a month later, I received notification from Police Headquarters that this summons was missing. This was a very serious matter. A frequent recurrence of "missing" summons could result in disciplinary action against me.

Because the summons was missing, I had to write a memorandum to give my explanation of why the summons was missing. I was angry. I knew what I saw happen, but I could not put that on paper. The truth was that the 5 Squad Officers had committed not only a departmental violation, but also a violation of the law. I was not about to climb that slippery mountain. In a "my word against his word" scenario, I felt I would lose. After all, he was part of the Captain's inner circle. My memorandum stated that I was not aware of what happened to the summons and that I would do all that I could to prevent a recurrence. Unfortunately, I wrote other violations on this vehicle and all disappeared and I had to write memoranda to try to explain why the summonses were missing. This was becoming a problem for me. I knew that the 5 Squad Officers were intercepting and destroying these summonses. I began a new personal policy for issuing summonses to Rocco Barba's vehicle. Instead of just writing the summons, I also documented the summons on a Police Incident Report. This was a matter of putting myself out of service for a few minutes, then asking Police Radio to assign a District Complaint number to this parking "investigation." This was never done by other Officers and it was not required. This was my way of documenting the issuance of the parking violation and insuring that this issuance and the summons number would be part of a document that would be permanently retained by the Police Department. In addition, I would write the number of the summons and the District Complaint number on my Daily Patrol Log and in my personal notebook. Subsequently, when I later received notification that a summons was missing, I would refer to these reports to verify that I had not only properly issued the summons, but also to whom it had been issued.

Over the period of several months, I was also able to garner information about Rocco Barba's involvement in illegal lottery and a burglary fencing operation. I learned that he stored a significant amount of stolen items in vacant properties he owned at 4322 and 4339 Main St. These properties were in the same block as the restaurant.

In approximately early January of 1977, the 5th Police District received a few new Officers from the recent graduates of the Police Academy. As was tradition, in the Police Department, these Officers were assigned to foot beats in business areas or were assigned to work with other Officers. On Sunday, February 1, during the 8am – 4:30pm shift, new Police Recruit C.C. was assigned a Foot Beat that included the 4300 Block of Main St. Officer C.C. was such a new Officer that I had not had time to have a discussion with him about the district and about Mr. Barba's activities.

At approximately 2:30pm, I was driving north in the 4200 Block of Main Street when I observed Police Officer C.C. walking northbound in the 4300 Block of Main Street. I, also, observed Rocco Barba standing in the middle of the street holding a parking summons and yelling at Officer C.C. "..You don't know who I am", he yelled. "I'll have your job for writing this ticket. I will be in the Captain's Office tomorrow morning." This was alarming. I sat and watched for a few seconds. After Rocco Barba had walked back into his store, I met with Officer C.C. to find out what had occurred. Officer C.C. stated that he had written a parking summons and placed it on the illegally parked vehicle outside of Mr. Barba's restaurant.

He did not know to whom the vehicle belonged. After he placed the summons on the vehicle, Rocco Barba emerged from the restaurant and began to berate him for writing the summons. Officer C.C. tried to explain that the vehicle was illegally parked and that he did not know that it belonged to someone in the restaurant. The vehicle was laden with trash and was in poor condition with an expired vehicle registration tag on it. He tried to explain this to Rocco Barba, but Barba was loud and angry. Officer C.C. walked away from the loud and angry Restaurant Owner. Now, I was angry. It was time to make the Captain aware of what I had learned about Mr. Barba's illegal activities. I accomplished this on February 3, 1977 at 9:30am.

Under normal circumstances, when an Officer wanted to report vice activity or other suspected criminal activity, he prepared a 75-48 (Incident Report). This report had three "tear off" sheets that were bluish gray (original top sheet), yellow (second sheet), and pink (third sheet). The Officer turned in the top two copies to either his Platoon Sergeant or the Operations Room Supervisor. The Officer retained the pink copy for his records. The remaining copies were supposed to be submitted to the District Commander (Captain). After the Captain received his copy, he was supposed to refer the information to the proper investigative agency.

As was normal, I arrived thirty minutes prior to the start of my shift. I used that extra time to prepare my report. I turned in the report to my Sergeant immediately after the 8:00am Roll Call. At approximately 9:15am, I received a radio call to report to the Captain's Office. A meeting this soon after submitting my report seemed unusual. When I arrived in Captain Simpson's Office, he was holding his copy of my report in his hand. His demeanor was very friendly. He asked about how I came about this information. I explained that I obtained it through extensive surveillance coupled with information I received from various members of the community. He pressed me to reveal the identities of the members of the community with whom I had spoken. I told him that all feared retaliation from either Rocco Barba or his agents. Because of that, I promised that I would not reveal their identities. After about fifteen minutes of discussion, he told me that he would have my information forwarded to the Commanding Officer of Northwest Police Division for further investigation. I thanked him as he ended our conversation. As I turned to leave the office, I had my "Colombo moment".

"By the way, Captain, yesterday Mr. Barba threatened an Officer for writing a summons on his illegally parked vehicle. I heard him tell that Officer that he was a "personal friend" of yours. Is that true?" The captain was cool as a cucumber. He responded, "I know Mr. Barba but if he is doing anything illegal, I will have the proper action taken. If you see anything illegal, you should take the proper action." His response was more assuring than I expected. As I left the Captain's Office, I was first grateful and relieved. Then, I wondered why a seemingly educated person would use a phrase such as "personal friend." I heard that term used a lot over my police career. Was there such a thing as an "impersonal friend"? By the nature of the word, "friend" has to be "personal." It was one of those stupid phrases people repeat over and over but it never made sense to me. It was comparable to saying "close proximity" which was the same as saying "near, near". All have become perpetual redundancy. My prep school English teachers would cringe at such poor English.

In the succeeding weeks, it was apparent that my report to the Captain had no effect. Very often, I would see an Officer from "Four Squad" enter the restaurant owned by Rocco Barba after his shift had ended. This Officer would walk into the restaurant with nothing in his hands and leave the restaurant with clothing or bagged items. He never carried food. Mr. Barba removed the expired tag from his illegally parked vehicle, but he did not move the vehicle. He continued to fill it with refuse. It remained parked in a bus stop. I continued to place summonses on the vehicle. All were removed by Mr. Barba or some other person.

My informants gave me the names of the men who were agents in Mr. Barba's illegal lottery franchise. Not only, was I given their names, but I was also given a description of the vehicles they used. One male, George, worked at the International Airport. He drove a 1972 Cadillac with Delaware registration. The other agent was Mark Grouper. He lived in the lower end of the 5th District on Manor St. With a suspended Driver's License, he drove a vehicle registered to a woman who lived in Southwest Philadelphia. I watched the actions of both men for several weeks on the day and evening shift. Both made predictable appearances at the restaurant owned by Mr. Barba. I wanted to be able to catch them with the illegal tools of their trade. I would have to either witness a transaction or see them carrying number plays with bets written on paper. In other busier districts, this type of surveillance by a uniformed Police Officer would be difficult. My sector was small enough and the service calls limited enough that I could devote extended observation time to suspicious activity without compromising sufficient and efficient patrol time.

Each Police District had a "Vice Book". Every Officer assigned to that district was responsible for reading this book to learn the identities of all of the "vice characters" in that particular district. This was always a huge concern of the Police Department. The book contained the arrest records and "mug shots" of all known persons in a Police District who had been arrested for crimes such as prostitution, illegal gambling, sale and/or use of illegal narcotics, and illegal liquor sales.

Once a year, each Officer had to submit a 75-48 which named a known vice offender in their district. I always disliked this report. It was almost useless. Almost every Officer went to the book to find the names they would submit for the annual report. Neither Rocco Barba nor his agents had their names in the book. When it came time to submit this report, I submitted Rocco Barba's name along with information about the crimes I alleged he was committing. Within one hour of submitting my report, Sergeant Val Spence, who was now my Platoon Sergeant, called for me to meet him in the district. Both he and the Corporal asked me why I had submitted a report on Mr. Barba. I told them that I had obtained my information from observations as well as information from confidential informants. In addition, I added that this was an addition to information I had previously submitted to our Captain. Both were very upset. They insisted on knowing my informants and wanted to know what credible information I had since Mr. Barba's name had never been turned in before. (In fact, no one had been arrested for illegal lottery in this district for several years.) I told them that I was building information that could possibly lead to Mr. Barba's arrest in the near future. The Sergeant tore up my report and told me to submit another one. He directed me to find a name in the "Vice Book". I complied. His behavior was distasteful. But he was my Sergeant. Insubordination was not the way to progress. Now, I was more determined to bring in more substantive information about Mr. Barba's criminal enterprise.

At the end of each shift, the squad reporting off would gather outside of the rear door of the district. Once the incoming squad finished Roll Call, the squad that was reporting off could enter and report off to their Sergeant. One morning, after ending the overnight shift, several Officers and I were standing outside waiting to report off. Someone began a conversation about "Rocky". I offered that I knew of criminal activity that was centered on "Rocky" and I was going to do my best to stop it in the near future. One Officer wanted to know what charges I would bring. I mentioned, that I had good information that Rocco Barba, was involved with illegal lottery, burglary, and possibly prostitution. I added that I knew that he had an expired Driver's License and that he, allegedly, sometimes carried a .22 caliber pistol without having a permit to carry a concealed deadly weapon. I told him it was just a matter of developing legitimate probable cause to take action.

Another Officer added, "If you are going to lock up 'Rocky', you are going to have to lock up half the cops in the 5th District." His quote was one that not only gave me chills but also aroused my ire. I countered, "Any cop that gets in my way will get arrested, too. You can be a cop or a crook, but you cannot be both." I was confident that my statement would be repeated to other Officers and would eventually make its way to "Rocky". I was correct.

Two weeks later, on Tuesday, September 27, 1977, I was working the day shift. About 10:30am, I parked my police vehicle almost directly across the street from the restaurant owned by Rocco Barba. I left my vehicle to make security checks on several businesses on Main St. I returned to my vehicle and began making entries on my Patrol Log. My peripheral vision picked up Mr. Mark Grouper, whom I suspected participated in Mr. Barba's illegal lottery enterprise. He exited the restaurant and walked towards my vehicle. I kept writing. He tapped on the window of my vehicle. I rolled down the window. He gave me the greeting of the day and introduced himself by first name. He stated that he had spoken with certain people in the Captain's Office and he was told that I participated in a lot of sports. He asked if I could use a couple of nice sweat suits. I thanked him, but told him that I was not interested. Internally, I was questioning why anyone in the Captain's Office would be discussing me with this civilian. Yes, I did participate in sports, but that should have never been something a person in the Captain's Officer should have revealed to him.

Sensing my irritation, Mark Grouper decided to get down to business. "Look my boss 'Rocky' is a nice guy. He has a lot of police friends and he wants to get along with everybody. It seems as though you and him got off on the wrong foot. He asked me to speak to you and maybe we can come to some sort of an agreement." Mark Grouper was nervously speaking with machine gun rapidity. He seemed a bit nervous. I was becoming a little uncomfortable with his standing next to my window. He was standing in the street. This was not a good position to be in when talking with someone whom you suspect was a criminal. I told Mark Grouper, who was 31 years old at this time that I was not interested in coming to any agreement with Mr. Barba. I added that if I saw either him or Mr. Barba engaged in illegal activity, I would arrest them. I tried to keep my tone mild. I told Mark Grouper to move away from the vehicle because I was about to drive off.

At this time, he leaned closer to the vehicle's open window. "Listen, my boss told me to give you this and maybe you will understand that he just wants to be your friend." With this, Mark Grouper dropped a large roll of money into my vehicle. The money fell to the floor. I never looked down. Mark Grouper began to walk away, I yelled, "Come back here!" He returned. "Look", I said, "I am going to open my door and I want you to take off the floor whatever you dropped in my car. If you don't pick it up, I am going to arrest you." He stated that I could keep it. I repeated verbatim my demand as I opened the door. Mark Grouper removed the roll of money and hurriedly walked back to the restaurant.

My heart was pounding. My blood must have been full of adrenalin. My hands were shaking. This had never happened to me before. What I did know, was that I needed to report this event as soon as possible. Without moving my vehicle, I asked for my Platoon Sergeant to meet me at the corner of Main and Cotton Streets. I found it odd and suspicious that in less than ten seconds after my call, Sergeant Val Spence appeared driving out of the unit block of Roxborough Ave. This street was just a few yards away from my location. This particular portion of Roxborough Ave, was only about 50 yards long, with very limited parking available. I wondered why he was there. Once he arrived, we moved our vehicles because there was not enough room for him to park. We parked a short distance away at Cresson and Levering Streets. I told him what had occurred. He did not appear to be surprised by this very unusual event. He wanted to know if I still had the money. I told him that I did not have it and that I never touched it. He wanted to know how much money the man gave me. I repeated that he never gave me the money. He dropped it through the window and I never touched it. The Sergeant signed my Patrol Log and told me to report the event to Lieutenant Clemens who was my Platoon Commander. I called for and met with the Lieutenant several blocks away near Main St. and Walnut Lane.

As I related this event to my Platoon Commander, he did not appear to be surprised. This was the second time in a very few minutes I had that same reaction. He appeared to be very uncomfortable with this conversation. He asked me why I had not arrested Mark Grouper. I told him that I did not make an arrest because Mark Grouper had never directly said that he wanted me to ignore any particular activity. He had been very careful with his words. Lieutenant Clemens thanked me for giving him the information. He never asked me to write a report about the event. I began to suspect that both he and the Sergeant were aware of Mark Grouper's behavior long before I called them. I suspected that this was a "set up". After all, with all of the area Sergeant Val Spence had as his responsibility, why was he sitting less than one hundred yards away while Mark Grouper had me involved in a conversation? Now, I knew that I could trust neither my Lieutenant nor my Sergeant. I surmised that they wanted me to take the money in order to either have evidence against me for bribery or to buy my silence on the activities of Rocco Barba.

On Friday, September 30, 1977, I was still working the day shift. In the early afternoon I was walking in the 4300 Block of Main St. making security checks of all the businesses. I nearly bumped into Mr. Mark Grouper as he was leaving a Jewelry Store in that block. Mark Grouper had a 5" x 7" piece of paper in his hand on which I could clearly see a list of three digit numbers with prices next to them. Mark Grouper quickly admitted that he was taking number plays. He had no fear because he probably had been doing this for a long time without interference from a Police Officer. He was surprised when I told him that I was placing him under arrest for taking illegal lottery bets.

I arrested him and called for an EPW to transport him to the district. Once I arrived at the district, everyone in the Operations Room seemed either hesitant or too busy to help me with the paperwork needed to process Mark Grouper. Within minutes, Lt. Clemens came into the district. He asked me about the arrest. Once he received my information, he became very nervous and told the Operations Room Team to expedite the paperwork. He told me that he wanted the paperwork done as quickly as possible before "anyone called and tried to get him released." He knew that if that situation evolved, it would become ugly very quickly in the district. He knew that I would be confrontational with anyone making such a request.

Within thirty minutes, the paperwork on Mark Grouper had been completed. His information was entered into the arrest book and he was quickly transported to the Police Administration Building for an Arraignment Hearing. During an arraignment, a Judge or Magistrate formally told the defendant of the charges against him. At this time, the Judge or Magistrate would notify the defendant of a Preliminary Hearing date and set bail, if required. The Judge or Magistrate, also, had the authority to dismiss charges. As Mark Grouper was being led from the 5th Police District's Operations Room, I told him, with my Lieutenant present, that his arrest was the first link in a chain that would lead to the arrest of his boss, Rocco Barba. Now, everyone in the 5th Police District, including Rocco "Rocky" Barba knew that I was serious.

A week later, as I was about to begin the 12am – 8am shift, a Police Officer from the squad that was reporting off stopped to speak with me. He, also, worked RPC 57 and he had been assigned to that car for several years. I thought he wanted to pass on information about some event that had occurred that evening. That would be normal. Instead, he began a conversation about "Rocky".

"It looks as though you and 'Rocky' have some misunderstanding. I just want you to know that I have known 'Rocky' for several years. He is a nice guy and he does not want any problems. He asked me to speak to you and maybe you guys can get together and have a conversation." I was dumbfound. First, an effort was made to bribe me, now a Police Officer was acting as an agent for "Rocky". I was disappointed in this Officer. He had almost twenty years of service on the department. I thought he was a good cop. I told the Officer that I was trying to do my job and that if I saw Mr. Barba or anyone else committing a crime, I was going to take the proper action. He shrugged his shoulders and walked away.

Now, it was time for the 5th Police District to retaliate against this Police Officer who was not willing to go along with their program. Frequently, I would report for my shift and would be told that I was going to be detailed to another district due to a staff shortage in that district. This should have been a rare occurrence, but it began to happen to me frequently. No one else in my district was ever told to leave and work in another district. This was designed to frustrate me. To make matters worse, during this time, I was having serious problems with my personal vehicle. The transmission was defective. I had to rely on public transportation to get to and from work. When these last minute assignments occurred, I had to take public transportation to those districts. Normally, this could mean an hour to ninety minutes of travel. Usually, by the time I arrived, the receiving district's supervisors had to make changes in order to find a place for me. They really did not need me.

Other times, I would find myself sent to various "Special Details" around the city. These details were normally assigned to Officers on a rotating basis. Under normal circumstances, a duty assignment register was kept and each Officer had an opportunity for assignment to these details. Those details covered large events that occurred at entertainment venues; the evening "bus detail" which had Officers "monitor" traffic on Broad St.; the 29th & Tasker Sts. detail to prevent racial violence in a playground in a racially sensitive area of South Philadelphia; and the infamous MOVE Detail in the Powelton Village section of the city.

At times, it became a bit of a joke because I became the only Officer in my platoon to be assigned to details. I remember one of the friendlier Officers in my platoon telling me about the Platoon Sergeant's assigning another Officer to a detail. Out loud the Officer protested, "Why are you sending me? Why aren't you sending Carter?" The Sergeant responded, "Carter is already on another detail." The platoon laughed. Very likely, I was assigned to the MOVE Detail, which required me to report to the Powelton Village site for a week. It was boring work. It involved standing outside in often inclement weather to hear a group of social misfits spew hatred and profanity over a megaphone in a residential area that was primarily populated by college students and college staff. A warrant had been issued for members of this group because they had threatened the lives of several government officials. They were armed with carbine rifles and other weapons.

Although many misguided politicians denied that this group was armed, I personally saw these weapons. At that time, two friends of mine and I were driving home via 34th Street when we saw the armed, militarily clad urban terrorists standing at "port arms" with their weapons. The cowards used their children as shields as they vowed to shoot anyone who tried to arrest them.

I was the designated detail man. I was the joke of my district. A popular singer by the name of Sam Cook had a song with the words, "I live on lonely island in the heart of the city." That was how I felt. "I might as well be shipwrecked in the middle of the sea." His song was about lost love. My experience was about my being ostracized in a public way for trying to stop criminal activity. I often sang that song to myself as I went from detail to detail. Music always had a calming influence on me.

My being assigned to every detail that was presented to the 5th Police District ended rather humorously. During the summer months, I was frequently assigned to security details at either Robin Hood Dell or the Mann Music Center. These were outdoor venues where free or very cheap musical concerts were performed. They were available to the general public and were always well attended. I enjoyed them because I had an opportunity to closely view such musical celebrities as Duke Ellington's Band, Sarah Vaughn, and many others. I enjoyed music. I enjoyed these details. One day, an Officer complained to my Lieutenant. He had been on an extended vacation. In recent years, he was always assigned the details to which I had been assigned. He told my Lieutenant that these were great assignments and he could not understand why he had been removed from being assigned to them. I never received details at those musical venues again. I found that to be amusing.

This was a difficult time for me. I had difficulty talking to anyone about what was occurring in the 5th District. My 2nd wife grew weary of my telling her about my daily exploits with my vindictive Supervisors. The few people who would listen to my venting, likely took me as being a bit strange. If so many cops were corrupt (their view), why was I acting like Cervantes' Don Quixote? Or was I like Diogenes walking against the wind with a wilting candle in my search for an honest cop? They listened, shook their heads, and sipped on another adult beverage. I found myself doing the same but not to any extreme that would keep me from work. The fact that I had seen my parents drown their frustrations in alcohol to the point they would call out sick from their jobs, kept me on the relative straight and narrow. My marriage fell apart partly because of the job and partly because I made some bad choices for "friends". We separated.

I found myself spending quiet days in an awful apartment in the East Oaklane section of the city. I found comfort watching sports, listening to music, and reading my Bible. Through them, I maintained my equilibrium. A few nights, when I was not working the next day, I would find a night club that played music and had dancing. I never frequented any place that was a "cop hang out." When I was not at work, I wanted to be totally away from the Police Department.

Outside of working, my only contact with Police Officers came through my activities with the Guardian Civic League. At this time, I was the Financial Secretary. As an elected official, I had opportunities to represent the GCL at many fund raising events. One of those events was a fund raising dinner sponsored by the Opportunities Industrialization Center (OIC) of Philadelphia. This organization was founded by Reverend Leon Sullivan in 1964. It was a non-profit organization that provided training for and employment of underprivileged men and women. Present day, this is an international organization.

I attended the fund raising dinner in either late September or early October of 1977. At the dinner, I was assigned to a table that had many high level city officials. It was my good fortune to have a seat next to a very prominent African American Federal Judge. First of all, I was in awe at sitting next to a man who was a living legend in the local African American Community. Secondly, while attending this gala event, I was still in mental turmoil. I wanted to resolve a situation that seemed to be too much for me to handle alone. Internally, I wanted to yell out to the world and tell them what I was going through. I could not write an editorial in the newspaper about this. I was frustrated. I was sitting next to a learned public official, but I did not want to burden him with my problem. Just because no one else listened, I should not make him a victim of my concerns.

Then, I remembered something from the Army. One of my barracks mates once said, "Faint heart never one fair lady." I was not trying to court a lady, but I did need to speak the concerns of my heart. The Judge and I had earlier engaged in small talk while eating dinner. As the event began to approach its end, I told him that I had a concern and I would like his opinion. In an abbreviated manner, I told him of the problems I was experiencing in the 5th Police District. His response was quick. He seemed to clearly understand what I was saying. He told me that he had to be cautious with what he was saying, but I should document everything I was experiencing. He further stated that I should continue to report any illegal activity I saw. The danger in not reporting it could place me in jeopardy of being thrown into the same pot as the people I was attempting to expose. Next, he said to make everyone over me accountable. This meant that when I did not experience a resolution of a concern, that I should pass that same information to the next higher person in rank. This takes away their ability to deny knowledge of any event. He stated I should start this process immediately. My soul felt unburdened. Now, I was certain that I was doing the right thing. Obviously, other eyes were looking into corruption within the Philadelphia Police Department. I needed to make it exceptionally clear that I was not a part of the problem. My mission was clear. Document and report. Document and report. Document and report.

My next step was to have the illegally parked vehicle removed. This had to be done surreptitiously because I had submitted several requests to have the vehicle removed and all were ignored. Over the years, I had assisted in preparing paperwork for arrests and for such things as abandoned vehicles. I had read the procedural directives for such tasks. I used this knowledge to take the next step of having the nuisance vehicle removed. I prepared most of the required paperwork at home. Unlike the typewriters at work, my personal typewriter only had a script font rather than the pica or elite fonts at work. I felt that this would not be a problem. Once completed, I had an Operations Supervisor from another squad sign the relevant paperwork. Rather than submit the paperwork to my Operations Team for processing, I hand-carried the paperwork to the Police Garage and gave it to a Supervisor one evening when I was off duty. I made sure to obtain the name of the person to whom I gave the paperwork. Now, it was time to wait.

On November 16, 1977, I worked the day shift. As normal, I made sure to check my very active business district in the 4300 block of Main

St. Unless there was a call for service, this was always my first check. That greenish blue Chevrolet that was parked in front of 4326 Main St. was gone. I was pleasantly surprised. My plan worked. Yippee for me and working outside of the box. I was overjoyed. This was progress. There was joy in my heart as I proceeded to make security checks of the businesses and the neighborhood.

Later in the day, I drove to the rear of the properties on the even numbered (west) side of the 4300 block of Main St. I had to enter from Cotton St. There, parked alone in a large seldom used lot, was that greenish blue Chevrolet packed with trash and garbage. The sinking feeling in my heart was barely exceeded by my rising temper. Seldom do I become angry. Today, I was angry. I looked for the first pay telephone I could find. The Supervisor to whom I gave the paperwork was working the evening shift. I had to wait until after 3:00pm to speak to him. I waited until after I arrived home to call him in the evening. After telling him what I had found, he stated he would contact the assigned Tow Truck Driver to find out what occurred. He asked me to call back in an hour. After waiting a bit more than an hour, I called and spoke to the Supervisor. The Tow Truck Driver told him that as he was preparing to tow the vehicle away, Restaurant Owner Rocco Barba confronted him. He told Mr. Barba that he had a written order to tow the vehicle and that Mr. Barba could recover the vehicle by contacting the Police Impoundment Lot. Mr. Barba walked back into the restaurant. As the Tow Truck Driver was driving south on Main Street with the trash laden vehicle, he was stopped by Sergeant Samples. Sergeant Samples was a Supervisor whom I had often seen going into Mr. Barba's restaurant during his off duty hours. He would often walk in with nothing and come out carrying either clothing or some other non-food item.

The Sergeant directed the Tow Truck Driver to place the vehicle in the rear of the restaurant. The Tow Truck Driver acquiesced but requested the Sergeant to sign his towing order. The Sergeant complied. I thought, "When will this nonsense end?" I thanked the Garage Supervisor for his information. He had no idea that I was steaming with anger. Now, I was focused on making all offending persons accountable. I remembered what the Federal Judge had told me. Document and report. Document and report. I had no idea of the dark path I would encounter as I embarked on this course of action.

The Dark Path

November 16, 1977 was my last day working Radio Patrol Car 57. I was
reassigned to Radio Patrol Car 513 which covered the Andorra section
of the 5th Police District. This sector was a few miles away from the sector
of Radio Patrol Car 57. Everyone had found out about the surreptitious
method I used to have "Rocky's" vehicle towed. I did not violate any
regulation or policy. I just went outside of their corrupt network. I was a
certified threat to the status quo.

On November 17, 1977, I prepared a memorandum directed towards
my Captain, the Inspector of Northwest Police Division, and the Internal
Affairs Bureau (Staff Inspectors' Headquarters). I wanted to insure that my
District Commander knew how I felt about his having ignored my initial
conversation with him about illegal activities emanating from Mr. Barba's
restaurant. In addition, I wanted to mention the complicit conduct of
Police Officers and Police Supervisors. I was through trying to be "Officer
Friendly". I closed the memorandum by saying, *"I feel this type of callous
disregard for the integrity of our office is a poor example to set for incoming
officers who joined the force."* I was trying to reach the tiny bit of decency
and integrity he may have had within him. I wanted him to know that I
was not afraid of the petty retaliatory tactics that had been and would be
directed towards me.

I waited for two days for a response from my District Commander
(Captain). There was none. One would think that the tone of my
memorandum would have had him jumping out of his seat with
indignation. I expected to be called into his office and receive some sort of
response. His ignorance gave me justification for proceeding to the next
level. On November 19, 1977, while at home, I prepared a memorandum

dated November 20, 1977. This later date would be the same day that I submitted it to my Commanding Officer for distribution to higher authorities in the Chain of Command. This memorandum detailed everything I knew about the illegal activities of Rocco "Rocky" Barba. This memorandum also noted that I had given information to my District Captain that had been ignored. I mentioned that Police Officers and Police Supervisors were protecting Mr. Rocco Barba. I mentioned the interference of a Supervisor in the removal of Mr. Barba's abandoned vehicle. I closed out the memorandum with the following:

> *"(8) That Mr. Barbera (sic) is engaged in criminal activity is fact, not imagination.*
>
> *That the integrity and credibility of the police officers in the 5th District have been extremely compromised by this aire of complacency and complicity is an unfortunate reality that must be corrected. We who honor our badge and realize our responsibility to the public do not need to have our integrity smeared by an individual who regards himself as the "Godfather of Manyunk." (It should have been Manayunk.)*

MEMORANDUM

POLICE
CITY OF PHILADELPHIA

DATE November 20, 1977

TO : Commanding Officer, Northwest Police Division

OM : Norman A. Carter Jr., Pol. #5246, 5th Police District

SUBJECT: Criminal Activity of Rocco Barbera

1. From approximately October 12, 1976 until November 16, 1977, I was assigned to radio patrol car "57". While assigned to this vehicle, I have become aware of criminal activity at 4326 Main St. This property, known as "Sip & Steaks Resturant", is owned and operated by Rocco Barbera, 49yrs, white male.

2. The property at 4326 Main St., is a three story brick edifice with the restaurant on the first floor, and apartments on the second and third floors. This restaurant is a front for a burglary fencing operation by Mr. Barbera. Mr. Barbera is also involved in illegal lottery violations, and may possibly be involved in loan sharking. I have also recieved information from many sources, whose information has so far proved to be very reliable, that Mr. Barbera is involved in the illegal sale of drugs.

3. The rooms above the restaurant have been used to consummate activities of prostitutes who work for Mr. Barbera. One of the girls employed as a prostitute who uses the premises is a seventeen year old white female. Another is a 23 year old white female known as Kathy Passalaqua.

4. Mr. Barbera is known as the man to see if one has stolen goods to get rid of. The stolen goods are stored either in the rear of the restaurant, or in a vacant ice cream store (owned by Mr. Barbera) at 4322 Main st. or in a Vacant store at 4339 Main St. The property at 4339 Main st., has a gate in front that is kept locked, even though two young ladies live in apartments above the first floor, and they must unlock the gate each time they leave or enter.

5. My reason for forwarding this information to your office is that on February 3, 1977, at 9:30 AM this very information was given to my captain, and in accordance with police department procedures, I submitted a copy of a 75-48 to him and discussed the matter with him. At this time he stated that information that was available to him, and veracity to the information that I had just given him, and that all of this information would be submitted to the commanding officer of the Northwest Police Division. In spite of the availability of all of this information, and inspite of numerous complaints recieved by me from residents and businessmen in the area, nothing has been done to curtail the activities of Mr. Barbera. The largest problem in dealing with Mr. Barbera is in dealing with the police officers and supervisors of the 5th District.

6. The captain, Captain ████████, informed me that he knew that Mr. Barbera was engaged in illegal vice activity, but, officers in the 5th District have never been instructed about not fraternizing with Mr. Barbera. As a result, I have seen a supervisor who frequents the establisment know as Sip & Steaks Restaurant while off duty, other supervisors engaged in jovial conversations in public with Mr. Barbera, and the captain's burglary team chauffering Mr. Barbera in their own vehicle while they were on duty.

7. Up until November 16th of this year, Mr. Barbera had an abandoned auto parked in front of his restaurant. He used this vehicle to store trash and garbage which was routinely picked up by a private garbage collector. I have written this vehicle up as abandoned no less that six times since last april. Absolutely no action was taken to remove this vehicle. On the sixteenth of November, I forwarded a memo to my captain, (a copy is enclosed), and the vehicle was moved within two hours by Mr. Barbera. It might also be noted that on September 14th of this year, I submitted a short memo to my captain concerning this vehicle, and there was no action taken. I have never recieved any information from the captain's office concerning this vehicle. A copy of this memo is also enclosed.

The First Interview at the
Internal Affairs Bureau

Within a few days, I received a phone call from Staff Inspector's Headquarters. I was told to come to that office to discuss the allegations made in my memoranda. On the afternoon of Tuesday, November 22, 1977, I went to the Internal Affairs Bureau (aka Staff Inspector's Headquarters) at 319 Race St. This was a very dreary looking building in a bleak part of the northeastern portion of Center City. (If you have ever seen the movie "Fallen" starring Denzel Washington, you have seen the inside of this location. This is where the Police Station sequences were filmed.) I went there alone in civilian clothing. Normally, Police Officers were told to have a Fraternal Order of Police representative with them whenever they were interviewed by a Staff Inspector. I saw no need to do this because I was a complainant. I would be interviewed by members of a unit with high integrity and whose job it was to investigate and eliminate corruption and poor practices by Police Officers. I was a bit nervous, but comfortable. First, I was greeted by Staff Inspector Cameron who had called me. He was Caucasian. His family was deeply rooted in the Law Enforcement Community of Philadelphia. He would be assisted by Staff Inspector Lassiter. I had never met him but had heard about Staff Inspector Lassiter. He was African-American and had been the Commanding Officer of a Police District in South Philadelphia. Many Officers spoke highly of him. I was becoming more comfortable. Both sat down with yellow legal pads.

Staff Inspector Cameron reminded me that this was a confidential investigation and that I should not share with anyone the content of this interview. He told me that his office would conduct this interview confidentially and that they would not reveal my identity to anyone. At the completion of their investigation, I would be contacted and given the results of their investigation. I was becoming more comfortable. I was only giving them facts and I did have some documentation. We discussed, in detail, every allegation I had submitted in my two memoranda. I was careful not to accuse any Police Officer of taking money or receiving other favors for their inaction. I did not have any empirical evidence of that. I was certain that a few Police Officers and Police Supervisors were complicit and facilitated illegal behavior by Mr. Barba. This interview took about two hours. As the interview ended, both smiled and shook my hand. Staff Inspector Cameron reminded me not to talk to anyone about this interview. I assured him that I would not. I left that building with a bounce in my step. I had reported that Police Officers, Police Supervisors, and my Captain were allowing a criminal enterprise to go unchecked. How could they not find that the information and documentation I had given to them were factual?

That night, I reported to work for my 12am – 8am shift. Working that first night of the "Last Out" shift was always tough. Everyone was usually a bit subdued in mood unless that first night was on the weekend. This was a mid-week night. As I walked in, that normal atmosphere of cordiality was gone. Officers looked and me and dropped their heads or turned away. I spoke, but no one spoke back. I found that strange. I went down to the locker room. The Officer a few feet away from me only grumbled when I spoke. What was going on? I tried to shrug it off. I was shocked when, at Roll Call, I was assigned to RPC 513 rather than RPC 57. No one was assigned to RPC 57. It was going to be left unmanned. This was highly unusual.

RPC 513's sector was in the quieter portion of the quiet district. I was told that I would be switched from the "B" platoon of my squad to the "A" platoon of my squad. I would be under a different Sergeant. Sergeant Waleski would be my Supervisor. I would still have the same Platoon Commander (Lieutenant). No one was making eye contact with me. I knew something was wrong. Someone had leaked that I had been to Internal Affairs. If it was not me, it had to be the Staff Inspectors with whom I spoke or my District Commander. Now, my comfort level was non-existent. I went out to my new assignment. I had to learn a new area.

A portion of my sector went into Wissahickon Park. Another portion was the very large and modern Andorra Shopping Center. I felt that I was figuratively banished to the biblical "Land of Nod". By the end of my tour week, I sensed that everyone in every squad knew that I had been to Internal Affairs. Almost no one, except three African American Police Officers in my squad, would speak to me. It was they who confirmed that there was a rumor that I had "ratted out every cop in the 5th District." That was not true, but that was the typical type of hyperbole that came with reliance on rumor rather than fact. It was, also, a strategy to isolate or ostracize the person providing the information. That person was me.

I could not understand why Officers whom I presumed to be honest and not involved with Mr. Barba would act this way. Peer pressure will often trump common sense. This was why cops, just like crime organizations, protected their own by keeping their mouths shut. If you want to be a part of "the team"; if you want to feel safe and know that you have support in dangerous situations; if you want to feel secure in your job and not have Supervisors and Commanders harass you then you keep your mouth shut no matter what indiscretions you witness or hear about other Officers. It was the "Code/Wall of Silence" sometimes known as the "Blue Wall" that must be maintained at all cost. I had cracked that wall. Now, it was time to eliminate that crack in order to prevent a greater fissure.

That night, my mind flashed back to that moment when I told a group of Officers "…either you are a cop or a crook. You cannot be both." I had, also said that I would do all that I could to see that Rocco Barba was arrested for his crimes and that any Police Officer who got between him and me may have to face consequences. I remembered the Judge who told me to document and report. I remembered the pledge I spoke when I was sworn in as a Police Officer. Nowhere in that pledge did it say that I should ignore illegal and immoral behavior of Police Officers. Nowhere in that pledge did it say that I should allow a criminal to evade punishment because he gave out free meals. Once you break the law you are no longer a Police Officer, you are a criminal. You go from capital letters and honor (Police Officer) to small letters and dishonor (criminal). I was not going to be a part of any cover up. If there were going to be consequences for practicing my belief, I was ready to face them. I remembered the corrupt cops that once patrolled the 23rd Police District in my North Philadelphia neighborhood. I remembered how much we who lived there did not have any respect for these Officers. That was not going to be me. I joined the Police Department to be part of changing that type of normality. But, keeping things in perspective, if my only penalty was changing my sector assignment, I could live with that. I was naïve. I was immensely naïve.

The Isolation Begins

The following week, I was working the 4pm – 12am shift. The ostracization was palpable. It was extreme. No one talked to me except the three aforementioned African American Police Officers. Even when they spoke to me, it was always in situations where no one else was around. They were all relatively new rookies with less than one year on the job. They feared for their jobs. I did not blame them for acting that way.

During the first or second day of this shift, I was making security checks in some of the stores in the Andorra Shopping Center. It was there I ran into my "Deep Throat." This was a coincidental meeting. This was a person who had unimpeachable information about what was going on in the 5th Police District. This was a person with whom I had rarely interacted. We were neither friends nor acquaintances. I was surprised when this person spoke to me. No one had initiated speaking to me in two weeks. This person began to walk with me as I left the store. Speaking in hushed tones, this person told me, "You need to watch your back. The Captain is very upset with you. Staff Inspectors came to visit him the other week. They were talking about you. Staff Inspector Lassiter (the African-American) walked into the Captain's Office and his first words were, 'How do we get rid of this mother…….' He was talking about you". My heart was pounding. Adrenalin must have been pouring through my arteries. I did not know what to say. "Please do not say you heard this from me." I told this person, whom I barely knew, that I would never betray them." Now, I felt alone. Truly alone. The Staff Inspectors had betrayed me. Instead of Rocco Barba and the complicit Police Officers being targeted, I was the target. I was the bad guy. It was my job and my career that were in jeopardy.

Two weeks later, I received a phone call at home from Staff Inspector Cameron. He told me that my allegations were thoroughly investigated and they could not be substantiated. He told me that he was closing the investigation unless I had additional information. I was disappointed, but not surprised. Now, I knew that the Internal Affairs Unit could not be trusted. I could only trust myself.

One evening, Sergeant Waleski was not working. Sergeant Spence, my former supervisor, was covering for him. As was normal, he called for me during the shift to meet with him so that he could sign my patrol log. We met on Ridge Ave. I left my vehicle and as was customary, I saluted him as I neared him. He was seated in his vehicle. He ignored my salute and dropped his head. I handed him the patrol log. He signed it, returned it to me, and drove away without saying a word. The next day, Sergeant Waleski was back to work. At some point in the evening we met so that he could sign my patrol log. After he signed my log, he told me that I had to submit to him a "memo" explaining why I had not saluted Sergeant Spence the previous day. I told him that I did salute him. In short, he told me to put that in my memo and to turn it into him the next day. I was dumbfounded. This Sergeant was lying and trying to discipline me for something I did not do. This was crazy. Still, there was nothing for me to do but to write the memorandum as requested. Of course, I denied that allegation without saying the Sergeant had lied. A week later, I was presented with disciplinary papers to sign. The papers were for insubordination by not saluting the Sergeant. This was super crazy. This had gone too far. In signing the paper, I had to indicate whether or not I was pleading guilty to the allegation. I indicated that I was not guilty. This meant that I would have a hearing before the Police Board of Inquiry (The Trial Board).

Shortly, thereafter I had to go to a hearing at the Police Board of Inquiry. This was a board comprised of several Executive Level Commanders and a minimum of one Police Officer of the same rank as I. This hearing was always held in the lower level of the Police Administration Building. I was nervous. While sitting in the waiting area, I was greeted by a lawyer who was hired by the Fraternal Order of Police. His job was to assist all Police Officers who arrived at the hearing. He had a copy of the charges against me. He stated that I should plead guilty. If I did this, he assured me that my most severe punishment would be a verbal reprimand. I refused this offer. I was innocent. Why should I plead guilty?

The hearing proceeded. A large reel to reel tape recorder was in operation throughout the hearing. The Sergeant testified. I testified and was asked questions. After my testimony had been completed, I was told that the board would vote on a recommendation. This recommendation would be passed on to the Police Commissioner for final approval. Once the Police Commissioner either approves or disapproves of their recommendation, they will notify both my Commanding Officer and me via mail. I left the hearing not feeling too confident.

In a few days my feelings were confirmed. I received a written reprimand. It stated that I had been found guilty and if I repeated the alleged behavior, I would be subject to further disciplinary action which could elevate to either suspension or dismissal. Now, they were establishing a paper trail that could lead to my being dismissed from the department. Now, as they used to say when I was in the Army, it was "time to soldier". The phrase "time to soldier" came from my experiences in the Army while stationed in the 37th Medical Battalion of the 5th Infantry Division. While there I became part of a group of seven African American soldiers. Racism was prevalent at our base located in Fort Carson, Colorado. We knew that to keep our supervisors from harassing us, we had to maintain ourselves and our equipment at the highest levels. Our uniforms were always immaculate. Our sleeping areas were always clean. We knew our General Orders because we tested each other. We obeyed all orders. We knew how "to soldier". This was now my circumstance in the Philadelphia Police Department's 5th Police District. It meant I had to be sure that every action I took had to be in accordance with proper procedure. My appearance had to be immaculate. I was walking on egg shells and still trying to protect the public.

Now, it seemed as though every week and sometimes every day, I was assigned to a detail that would keep me out of the district. Only on weekends or on the overnight shift could I be almost certain that I would work in the district. This was harassment at the highest level. I did not complain, but this became ponderous if not overwhelming. I actually began to get ill. Whenever I walked into my district, I could feel my stomach turning over. Whenever I spoke with a Sergeant or Lieutenant,

I had to speak carefully. I trusted no one. When I was given assignments that required two or more Officers, no one would assist me. If the Police Radio Dispatcher tried to assign another Officer to assist me, they would not answer immediately. If they did answer, they would never arrive. The entire Northwest Police Division knew that I was a man on Ostracization Isle. The waters around this island were filled with sharks who would attack anyone who entered those waters to assist me. I was the Poster Boy for what happens to anyone who "rats out cops". I was a traitor. One way or another, I was going to be eliminated.

For a few sentences let me try to explain something important. A good many Police Officers in the 5th Police District, during my tenure there, viewed me as a "rat". The use of that terminology was totally inaccurate. According to the vernacular of that time, a "rat" was a person/criminal/Police Officer who was involved in illegal activity. Once that person was arrested, if he gave information on his partners in crime in order to gain favor with the Prosecuting Attorney, he would be dubbed a "rat". I was not involved in any criminal enterprise. I either saw or was informed of behavior that if it was not outside of the law it was certainly outside of proper police procedures. I reported what I observed. That does not make me a "rat". But, if one joined the throng that was dubbing me thusly, it was purely part of the peer pressure that outsiders view as the "Blue Wall". As difficult as it may be to pierce this wall from the outside, imagine how difficult it was working inside of this oppressive environment.

I called the Fraternal Order of Police. Surely, they could help me. The representative I spoke with clearly told me that because I was making accusations against Police Officers, they could not support me at the same time they might have to defend the other Officers. If you cannot depend upon the bargaining unit to whom you are paying dues, then you are in a very bad place physically and emotionally.

In two weeks, Sergeant Waleski approached me again. He tells me that I need to submit a "memo" because Sgt. Spence reported that he saw me walking outside of my vehicle without my hat. Police Department regulations required that you wore your hat whenever you left your vehicle. (This policy changed when women began to be assigned patrol duty in the Police Department.) This allegation was preposterous. I had never left my vehicle without wearing my hat. The Sergeant clearly lied, again.

I wrote a memorandum and explicitly stated that the Sergeant was lying. That is a dangerous thing to do, but I felt no need to mollify my outrage. I had asked for help from the Fraternal Order of Police and was denied. I had spoken to members of the Guardian Civic League about my predicament. Several members laughed at me when I explained that the impetus for the actions of the Captain and Police Officers of the 5th District was that I had exposed activities that were malfeasant at best and possibly corrupt. That really hurt. Therefore, my only weapon was the truth. Putting in writing that my Sergeant was lying was the only option left to me. He was trying to get me fired. I was trying to survive and keep my career. Aren't good guys supposed to win? I was not feeling that way.

Several days passed and there was no response to my memorandum. The allegation disappeared. No one told me this, but I am sure someone figured out that the Sergeant had gone too far. Still, the harassment continued. I was constantly being sent out on details away from the district. Many times, the car I was assigned to was put out of service and I would be assigned a foot beat. One day shift, it became ridiculous. I believe it was a very cold day in February. I was assigned to a foot beat in a residential area. The foot beat was from the 4000 block to the 4200 block of Terrace St. Except for a store which sold furs and a small candy store the area was all residential. No one had ever been assigned to that beat. It was cold and there was no place to either get warm, go to the bathroom, or to have lunch. This was not about crime prevention. It was about punishment.

Sergeant Val Spence rode by frequently to make sure I was on my beat. Where could I go? The next day, I was assigned to the same beat. Because no one would take me to the beat and because there was no public transportation to take me to the beat, I walked about two miles up and down the hills of Manayunk to the beat. The good part about walking was that my long underwear and leather top coat generated and held my body heat as long as I kept moving. On this second day, it was still cold but things got a little better.

A middle-aged Caucasian lady opened her door as I was walking in the 4000 block of Terrace St. She was very happy to see me. She stated that she rarely saw a Police Officer on her block and that she had never seen one walking a beat in this block. She thanked me for being there.

She asked me if I wanted coffee or something to eat. Those who know me know that I am very funny about food. My knee jerk answer would be to politely refuse, but I thought acceptance would be a good way to establish a relationship with that community. My thinking was that I would likely have this beat many times in the future. I accepted the offer of coffee. She asked me to stop back in fifteen minutes. I returned and stood in her doorway. We were letting out all of her precious heat while I was sipping on a cup of well appreciated coffee. She continued to praise the 5th District for assigning me to this beat. I did not dampen her pleasure by telling her that this was the district's way of punishing me. It was a good moment. The next day, my assignment was changed.

I was assigned to a foot beat in the Andorra Shopping Center. Again, my patrol car was put out of service for no reason. Again, I was put on a foot beat that was never assigned to anyone else. Again, I could not obtain a ride to my assignment that was about two miles away. One was not allowed to take one's personal vehicle to an assignment. This time, I waited for a SEPTA bus (the public transit authority for Philadelphia) which took me to within a short distance from my assignment. I, actually, enjoyed the assignment.

There were dozens of businesses. It seemed as though everyone appreciated seeing a Police Officer walking pass their windows. Although I felt ostracized by my co-workers, I never felt that treatment from the community. Although, I could never prove it, I believe this business community began to call the district and voiced compliments about my being there. You must remember, the last thing the Management of the 5th Police District wanted was community and business support for me. They wanted me gone. They wanted me to either resign or be fired. After a couple of days, I was back in RPC 513.

This banishment, may have been viewed as punishment by my superiors, but I found a way to make it work for me. This car received very few calls for service. Therefore, I did not have to worry about Police Officers interfering with my radio transmissions. As with every assignment, I made it a point to know the people in the community. This happened when I parked my vehicle and walked around. The public appreciated the security of seeing a Police Officer in their neighborhood. This was a middle income to upper middle income neighborhood. People wanted to feel confident that their homes and assets were protected. These people talked to me. Oddly, it seemed as though many of these people who lived miles away from Main Street still harbored strong feelings about the illegal activities that were headquartered at Rocky's restaurant. In addition, some voiced their distrust of the 5 Squad Police Officers who were frequently seen with owner Rocco Barba. My conversations with some of these citizens directed my attention to the man who was not only closely associated with Mr. Barba, but also with Mayor Frank L. Rizzo. This political person was a heavy contributor to the Mayor's Election Campaign.

What I learned from the community but could not verify was that this person served as a conduit between Mr. Barba and the Mayor. The "word on the street" was that Mr. Barba had contributed thousands of dollars to the Mayor's first election and to his re-election campaigns. The money was given to this politician who funneled the money to the Mayor's campaign organization. I, was truly fighting City Hall. Rocco Barba was invincible.

During this time, my informants who lived and worked in the area of Mr. Barba's restaurant continued to give me information about the activities of Mr. Barba. It was somewhat frustrating. I was not working in the area, but these people were looking for relief from the burglaries, the prostitution, the illegal lottery, and the less than vigilant Police Officers. They trusted me to do something.

I began to organize all of my documentation. Rocco Barba and his legion of criminals had to be stopped. It was time to go back to the typewriter. It was time to develop a strategy that could not be blocked by Rocky's minions who were working in the 5th Police District and the Northwest Police Division. In order to protect myself while pursuing the unravelling of Rocco Barba's mini-empire I had to document that I had used every resource available to me. That meant taking away any avenue of deniability for all in my Chain of Command. It meant systematically making everyone from the Operations Room Corporal to the Mayor of Philadelphia aware of what was occurring in the 5th Police District. This was not an easy task because I knew that my Captain and probably the Inspector of the Northwest Police Division would block the normal flow of information upward. My goal was not to punish Police Officers. It was to arrest a criminal who was having a severely negative impact on the communities of Manayunk, Wissahickon, Roxborough, and Andorra. These were all communities within the 5th Police District. Still, one must always remember that I told a group of Police Officers in my squad that any Police Officer who took it upon himself to run interference for Rocco Barba was not a cop but a crook.

The Suspended Driver's License Saga

It had to be late October 1977 when I received a notice from the State Bureau of Motor Vehicles that because my vehicle registration had expired, by Operator's License would be suspended, almost immediately. This did not make sense. My vehicle registration was up to date. It took a couple of days before I could send a letter to the Bureau questioning their conclusion. The following week, I received a letter stating that they had committed an error. My Operator's License would be restored immediately and no further action would be required on my part.

A few weeks later, there was a snow storm. It was my day off. There was a knock at my apartment door. It was a Lieutenant from the 5th Police District. This was unusual. He had driven nearly ten miles in deep snow. He stated that he came to serve me with disciplinary papers because my Operator's License was suspended. I had to sign the papers (form 75-18) and I would have to appear at a Police Board of Inquiry Hearing the following week. In the meantime, I was suspended because I could not drive legally. I was shocked. The Lieutenant explained that the Police Department received alerts whenever a Police Officer's Operator's License was suspended or revoked. I signed the form and told the Lieutenant that I was certain my license was valid. I, purposely, did not share with him the fact that I received a letter stating the Bureau of Motor Vehicles had made an error and had corrected that error. Fortunately, the hearing was schedule soon. I missed only two days of work.

I came to the hearing with my documentation. The Fraternal Order of Police always had a lawyer present to assist and advise any Police Officer who comes before the board. The grim faced lawyer approached me. He probably felt that I was on my way either out of the department or would have a prolonged suspension. As with my appearance at an earlier hearing, he suggested that I plead guilty. I refused his suggestion. I was not guilty of anything. Any lawyer who continually recommended that you plead guilty was not working on your behalf.

I sat down before the board which was comprised of about four Command Level Officers and one peer Officer. There was a large tape recorder sitting at the far end of a long table. The entire proceeding was to be recorded. This was normal.

The leading Officer asked me to explain the reason my license had been suspended. In addition, he asked for my reason in not notifying the department of the suspension. I told him that the Bureau of Motor Vehicles had made an error and that my license was valid. He debated that point with me by citing a report he had in his hand. At this point, I presented him with the letter I had received from the Department of Motor Vehicles. His faced turned pale. "Why didn't you give this to the Lieutenant when he served you with the papers?" I told him that I did not trust anyone in the 5th Police District. I told him that I felt the letter would disappear.

Then he asked, why didn't I give this form to the District Captain? I told him that the Captain did not talk to me. He asked why. I told him that I would rather not answer that question in this forum. The Commander and several others demanded that I tell them why the Captain would not talk to me. Reluctantly, I stated, "The Captain does not talk to me because I have made allegations that he and other Officers are protecting a criminal in the 5th District." The Lead Commander directed that the tape machine be turned off. This Commander lectured me that I should have notified someone about this error. It would have prevented time wasted on this hearing. I verbally agreed with him although I was telling myself that there was no one I could turn to that I trusted. I did what was right for me at the time. I wanted to present my letter at a taped meeting among several witnesses. Here, with several witnesses, I felt protected. The truth could not be torn up and thrown away. I walked away with no loss of pay. The charge against me was dropped. I was vindicated......this time.

It's A Dangerous Job

Throughout most my time in the 5th Police District, I was seldom backed up by another Police Officer when making a vehicle investigation, pedestrian investigation, or other assignments which normally required the presence of two Police Officers. I did not allow the behavior of others to dictate how I did my job. My military background trained me to always do my job the way it was supposed to be done. I had to "soldier on." Even when others were less responsible or less vigilant, I always did my job properly. To not do so could jeopardize my life or the lives of others. This truly came to reality one autumn evening near 9:00pm.

I was patrolling my sector in 513 car when another 5th District Police Officer notified Police Radio that he was stopping a vehicle for investigation in the 7900 block of Henry Ave. This location adjoined my sector. Immediately, I notified the Police Radio Dispatcher that I would drive over to back up this Officer. This would have never happened had the situation been reversed. I arrived at the location just as the Police Officer was leaving his vehicle to walk up to the driver he had stopped.

As was customary when stopping a vehicle, the Police Officer had notified the Police Dispatcher of the vehicle's description and its tag number before he left his vehicle. The Officer later related to me that as he approached the vehicle's driver, he saw the driver bend over shortly after I arrived. The Police Officer asked the driver for his Operator's License and vehicle registration card. He informed the driver that he stopped him because he had driven through a red stop signal. The driver gave him the requested papers. As the Police Officer walked back to his vehicle, an Emergency Alert Signal preceded the Police Dispatcher's high pitched excited voice. "All cars stand by. Police Radio to 512". This was an indication that something was very wrong.

"512, go ahead radio", the Officer responded.

"The Operator of the vehicle you have stopped is wanted for a holdup point of gun in Lower Merion Township. Do you have back up with you?"

"Yes, 513 is with me."

"Use caution, this male is armed."

I alit from my vehicle and walked to the passenger side of the vehicle with my flashlight focused on the driver's head. There was no other occupant of the vehicle. The other Police Officer asked the driver to step out of the vehicle. The driver complied. Without incident, he handcuffed the driver and placed him the back seat of his patrol car. Then, the Officer went back to the stopped vehicle to make a cursory check of the vehicle's contents. He could clearly see the hand grips of a pistol partially placed under the driver's seat of the vehicle. He gently removed the pistol and notified Police Radio that the perpetrator and the weapon had been retrieved. The pistol was a long barreled, silver plated gun that was too large to fit under the seat of the car. An Emergency Patrol wagon arrived to transport the prisoner. I returned to my normal patrol. My shift ended a few hours later, and I reported off as normal.

The next day, I was seated in front of my locker prior to the beginning of my shift. There were no other Police Officers in the room until the Officer who had made the arrest the night before arrived. He walked towards me. His eyes were mainly focused on the floor. It was almost as if he felt guilty about something. When he was close to me, he looked up and in an almost whispered voice said words similar to, "I just want to thank you for backing me up. As you were driving up, that guy bent over. He must have been putting the gun under his seat. I think he did that because he saw you coming. I don't care what other's think about you, I appreciate what you did last night." I was almost speechless. I thanked him for the compliment. It was the first time that an Officer had spoken to me in weeks. It highlighted in his mind and in mine that we had a dangerous job and you could lose your life in an instant if we did not work together as a team. Still, everyone else treated me the same as usual. I am not sure that this Officer shared his gratitude for my actions with other Officers. That sharing was not important. What was important was that he appreciated what had occurred. Had I acted as irresponsibly as my co-workers, this vehicle investigation could have turned out much differently.

The Fur Store Caper

On or about late October 1977, my last day on the day shift tour, I read the Part One Sheet before Roll Call. A Furrier located in the 4000 Block of Terrace St. had been burglarized the night before. Several thousands of dollars in furs had been taken. As punishment, I had been assigned the beat on which that furrier was located a few weeks before. This Furrier was located in a highly populated, predominantly residential neighborhood. On this day, I was assigned to Radio Patrol Car 513 on a sector that was miles away from the Furrier.

The next evening at about 8:30pm, I received a phone call from one of my informants. The informant asked if I had heard about any stolen furs. I responded that I did know about such a burglary. The informant had gone into Rocky's restaurant earlier in the evening. The informant stated that Rocky was showing customers furs that he was selling at discounted prices. The furs were stored in a closet inside of the restaurant. The informant further stated that the furs still had tags on them indicating they belonged to the Furrier on Terrace St. The informant told Rocky that he/she might return later if he/she could come up with the money to purchase a fur coat.

I called a second person who had given me reliable information in the past. This business person stated that several customers were speaking of furs being sold in Rocky's restaurant. This person had not seen the furs. I felt I was developing credible enough information to establish probable cause for a Search Warrant. I was due to report in for the overnight shift that night. I felt a sense of urgency to catch Rocky with these furs. My only problem was that I knew that I would not be working in that area. I was likely going to be assigned to Radio Patrol Car 513. Ideally, a Search Warrant would be strengthened if I could apprehend someone walking out of the restaurant with a fur coat. Based on past behavior, I knew that I could not trust any Police Officer in the 5th Police District to make a credible surveillance of the restaurant. All Police Officers in that District viewed Rocco "Rocky" Barba as an "untouchable".

I went through the Police Department's Procedural Directives I had at home and reviewed the process for obtaining a Search Warrant. I would have to complete a worksheet and have this approved by my Platoon Commander, then take it to the Northwest Detective Division. After that, it would have to be approved by a District Attorney and signed by a Judge. About 9:45pm, I called my informant to ask him/her to return to the restaurant to insure that the furs were still there. In thirty minutes, I received a call back that the furs were still there. I was already dressed for work. I left immediately and arrived about 45 minutes before the beginning of my shift.

On arrival at the Police Station, I walked directly into the Operations Room. I took two copies of a Search Warrant Work Sheet. I took them down to the locker room and began to complete all of the required information. I told no one what I was doing. After Roll Call, I approached my Platoon Lieutenant. It was very unusual for a uniformed Police Officer to apply for a Search Warrant. I caught him completely off guard. He read the form. He asked for the names of my informants. This was a bad request. A Police Officer was never obligated to release the name of informants. With all of the harassment that I was receiving as a Police Officer, how would informants be treated? I politely refused to name my informants. His next question concerned how I was getting information from informants when I was no longer working in that area. I told him that my informants trusted me and did not trust that other Police Officers would use the information properly. There was joy in my heart as the Lieutenant approved my taking the worksheet to the Northwest Detective Division.

On my arrival to the Northwest Detective Division, I met with a Detective Sergeant. He read my worksheet. He questioned me about my informants. Again, I refused to give him the names. I did inform him that my informants were reputable members of the community and that they had given me reliable information in the past. After about a fifteen minute discussion, he informed me that his detectives were too busy to type up a Search Warrant. It might take a few hours before one could take the time to review my worksheet and type the warrant. I told him that I was fully capable of typing the warrant. All I required was the proper form and a typewriter. The Detective Sergeant did not know I was a touch typist who could type better than fifty words per minute. It took me about twenty minutes to complete the warrant as I had to prepare it on the worse typewriter in the office.

After completing the warrant, I had to wait about thirty minutes before the Detective Sergeant would review and sign the warrant application. I began to feel a little uneasy. This seemed to be an odd delay. No one seemed to be that busy. After he approved and signed the warrant, I had to drive eight miles to the Police Administration Building (PAB) at 8th and Race Sts. In order to have the Search Warrant approved and signed by a Judge.

The Night Arraignment Court was located on the first floor. There was always an Assistant District Attorney and a Judge available there. At the time of my arrival, about 1:45am, there were no arraignments in progress. Still, it took thirty minutes before the Assistant District Attorney met with me. When I met with him, he appeared to be very irritated. Maybe, it was the hour of the morning. Maybe, he had a bad day. I presented the warrant to him. He appeared to give it a cursory glance, but seemed to be aware of all the details. "Who are your informants?" I told him that I could not reveal their names because of my concern for their safety. "What kind of information had they given you in the past?" I told him about an arrest I had made for illegal lottery. In the nastiest of tone, he told me that I did not have enough probable cause and he would neither approve the warrant nor present it to a Judge for signing. I was emotionally crushed. I had just spent nearly four hours, which was an inordinate amount of time, preparing and presenting this warrant. I knew the furs were sitting in the restaurant. How could he disapprove my warrant?

On my long drive back to the 5th Police District, I began to replay all of the events that transpired that night. The long delays at both Northwest Detective Division and at the PAB were unusual. There was no urgency. Thousands of dollars in furs being easily accessible in a restaurant and there was no urgency. There was not even a suggestion by the Detective Sergeant or the Assistant District Attorney that either I or another Police Officer conduct further surveillance at the restaurant. On my return to the borders of my district, I put myself back in service via two-way radio. It was about 4:15am. My Sergeant immediately called for me to meet him on my sector in order for him to sign my patrol log. There was minimal information on my patrol log as I had spent the entire shift attempting to have the Search Warrant approved and signed. I told him that the warrant was not approved. He did not seem to be surprised. I went on to complete my shift.

Shortly, after I arrived at home, I received a call from one of my informants. The conversation went something like this:

Informant: "I bet you didn't get anything out of Rocky's."

Me: "No, they wouldn't approve my Search Warrant. I took it down to the District Attorney, but he refused to sign it."

Informant: "Well, I was standing outside of Rocky's with a friend of mine about twelve o'clock (midnight). All of a sudden, Rocky and some guys started taking the fur coats out of the closet. They put some of them in the trunk of a car and some in that vacant store across the street.

               They were moving fast."

Me: "Now, I understand. Someone from either the 5th District or Northwest Detectives called Rocky."

Now, I understood the delays. Now, I was certain that Rocky's influence went as far as Northwest Detective Division. The problem appeared to be larger than I had expected. I had one more avenue of redress. That avenue ran directly through my family. Years ago, while I was working in the 14th Police District, I worked with an Officer, who was now working with a major investigative agency within the Police Department. He was the cousin of my 2nd wife. His agency was part of a task force that was in the process of rooting out major theft and drug organizations operating in Philadelphia. During the late 1970's the Philadelphia Police Department had been targeted for several investigations by both State and Federal Law Enforcement Agencies. Philadelphia Police Officers were brainwashed into not trusting any law enforcement agency outside of Philadelphia Police

Department. The investigative agency my wife's cousin was a part of had Pennsylvania State Police Investigators working with them.

Mayor Frank L. Rizzo was the catalyst for this schism between law enforcement agencies. Mayor Rizzo's proclamations about being tough on criminals masked what went on behind the scenes. Most of the city forgot that Mayor Rizzo's first act after becoming Mayor was to grant a zoning variance to a member of the South Philadelphia branch of the Mafia. This variance allowed this criminal to open a business in an area where he had been denied in previous years because of his criminal background. When questioned about his giving preference to a Mafia member, Frank Rizzo, the proclaimed bastion of firm law enforcement proclaimed, "There is no such organization as the Mafia." Such a stupid statement from a former Police Commissioner should have brought both alarm and laughter. Oddly enough, former Federal Bureau of Investigation Director J. Edgar Hoover made a similar statement early in his career. Surely the Mayor must have been joking. Unfortunately, Frank Rizzo was such a dominating and feared personality that most citizens and news reporters were reticent to challenge him on anything. Once Rizzo challenged a Television News Reporter to a fight because he did not appreciate being questioned about a particular issue. It was common knowledge that Mayor Rizzo kept dossiers on people who disagreed with him. He used Police Officers that should have been investigating crimes to compile this information. This was the same pattern of behavior used by FBI Director J. Edgar Hoover and other political bullies whenever they felt their authority was being challenged. If you did not respect him, he wanted you to fear him. I felt that my actions were about to have my name placed on Mayor Rizzo's "Enemies List." Such would be my reward for interfering with a criminal operation.

Turning the Wheel of Justice

It has been often said that the wheel of justice turns slowly. Still, it turns and gradually moves to crush the unjust. On March 16, 1978, I prepared a two-page memorandum that was to be submitted, through channels, to the Major Investigations Unit of the Chief Inspector of the Patrol Bureau North. I trusted the Chief Inspector of the Patrol Bureau North. I knew that I would have to use both departmental and surreptitious channels to insure that this memorandum reached the desired destination. I turned the memorandum into my District Commander. In addition, I contacted a cousin by marriage who worked in the Major Investigations Unit. I told him that I expected that my original memorandum would be trashed before it arrived to his unit. We had a long discussion about the need for the utmost in confidentiality because not only were Police Officers running interference for Rocco Barba's criminal enterprise, but also some Detectives in Northwest Police Division.

My memorandum mentioned the juvenile and persistent retaliation I experienced after I reported the misconduct of certain Police Officers in the 5th Police District. I mentioned that Rocco Barba's cohorts stored stolen good in vacant properties at 4322 Main St. and 4334 Main St. These vacant storefronts were owned by Rocco Barba. I told this Police Officer that he and his unit could not trust anyone associated with the Northwest Police Division. He assured me that he would do whatever he could. It would be almost a year before I found out the results of his labor. I will discuss the resolution as it evolved later in this treatise.

The Performance Evaluation

Each year, a Police Officer received a written Performance Evaluation. This evaluation was normally prepared by one's Platoon Sergeant and co-signed by one's Platoon Lieutenant. Throughout my previous ten years of service, my performance evaluations received ratings of either "Satisfactory" or "Outstanding". My Performance Report for Permanent Employee received in May of 1978 was a sad harbinger of things to come. My overall rating was "Unsatisfactory".

It began with a self-indictment of some of the treatment I had been receiving. "During the time you have been under my Supervision you continuously when given details at Move & 29th * Tasker St. Detail & Parade Details, you have reported Off Sick, indicating that when you receive an assignment not to your liking, you have reported off sick."

It added that I did not communicate well with my fellow Officers. He failed to note that they were the ones who stopped speaking to me. In addition, they were the ones who interfered with my radio transmissions. I expressed my displeasure about the inaccuracy of the report. Sergeant Spence's reply was "The very next thing you do, I am going to take you to the front". ("The Front" was police jargon for preferring charges against an officer for violations of policy or procedures.)

This was a threat to bring disciplinary charges against me. He had no basis for the charges. This was his knee-jerk reaction to being confronted about an unfair and untrue characterization of my job performance. It is important to note that I had not been working under this Sergeant's supervision for several months. This was a conspiratorial act committed in concert with my Lieutenant and the District Commander (Captain). Obviously, my current Platoon Sergeant, Sergeant Waleski, opted out of participating in this attempt to derail my career.

Norman A. Carter Jr.

PERFORMANCE REPORT FOR PERMANENT EMPLOYEE

			RECEIVED	PRINTED
			19	19

NAME (Last)	(First)	(Initial)	PAYROLL NUMBER	SPECIAL	X ANNUAL
CARTER JR	NORMAN	A	108188		

CITY DEPARTMENT	DEPARTMENT NO.	ANNUAL RATE	INCR. DATE MO. DAY	TYPE APPT	DEPT AKET DATE OF REASN
DISTRICT 5	11-AA-85-05	16,024	03/00	111-1	07/17/78

CIVIL SERVICE TITLE	CLASS CODE	RANGE	STEP	ORIGINAL APPT MO. DAY YEAR
POLICE OFFICER	6A02	03	4	03/20/67

COMMENTS TO EMPLOYEE

XXXXXXXXXXXXXXXXXXXXXXXXXXXXXXXXXXXXXXXXXXXXXXXXXXXXXXXXXXXXXXXXXXXXXXXXXXXX
XXXXXXXXXXXXXXXXXXXXXXXXXXXXXXXXXXXXXXXXXXXXXXXXXXXXXXXXXXXXXXXXXXXXXXXXXX
XXXXXXXXXX During the time you have been under my Supervision you continuously
when given details at Move & 29th & Tasker St. Detail & Parade Details, you
have reported Off Sick, indicating that when you receive an assignment
not to your liking, you report off sick. I, therefore rate you Unsatisfactory
in this Category, Dependability. During the past year I have been approached
by fellow Policemen in the Squad who have worked ajoining sectors with you
and they have requested other assignments due to your incomplete messages
on Radio and your lack of communication with them. I rate you Unsatisfactory
in the category, Relationship with people.

For your information I have summarized my best judgment of how well you have performed the duties of your position during the period covered since your last report. A duplicate copy of this report is being forwarded to the Personnel Department.

RATINGS ARE INDICATED BY "X" MARKS

	PERFORMANCE FACTORS	UNSATISFACTORY	IMPROVEMENT NEEDED	SATISFACTORY	
1	QUALITY OF WORK — Accuracy; precision; completeness; neatness. (Quantity not considered.)			X	
2	QUANTITY OF WORK — Amount of work turned out. (Quality not considered.)				
3	WORK HABITS — Organization of work; care of equipment; safety considerations; promptness; industry.			X	
4	RELATIONSHIP WITH PEOPLE — Ability to get along with others; effectiveness in dealing with the public, other employees, patients or inmates.	X			
5	INITIATIVE — Self reliance; resourcefulness; willingness and ability to accept and carry out responsibility.			X	
6	DEPENDABILITY — Degree to which employee can be relied upon to work and to meet deadlines without close supervision.	X			
7	ANALYTICAL ABILITY — Thoroughness and accuracy of analysis of data, facts, laws and rules.				
8	ABILITY AS SUPERVISOR — Proficiency in training employees, in planning, organizing, laying out and getting out work; leadership.				
9	ADMINISTRATIVE ABILITY — Promptness of action; soundness of decision; application of good management principles.				
10	FACTORS NOT LISTED ABOVE: (Use additional sheets, if needed.) PROMOTIONAL POTENTIAL	X			
	OVER-ALL RATING: Must be consistent with the factor ratings, but there is no prescribed formula for computing the over-all rating.	UNSATISFACTORY		SATISFACTORY X	

SIGNATURE OF RATER	TITLE Sergeant #	DATE 5-17-78

I WOULD LIKE TO DISCUSS THIS REPORT WITH THE REVIEWING OFFICER.	IN SIGNING THIS REPORT I DO NOT NECESSARILY AGREE WITH THE CONCLUSIONS OF THE RATER Signature of Employee	Date 5-17-78
AS REQUESTED, REVIEWING OFFICER DISCUSSED REPORT WITH EMPLOYEE ON (Date)	I CONCUR IN THE RATINGS GIVEN BY THE RATER. I HAVE MADE NO CHANGE IN THE REPORT Signature of Reviewing Officer	Date 5-17-78

3-28 (Rev. 10/68)

Unlike many Police Officers, I knew that I could submit a challenge to this Performance Evaluation and have it placed in my Personnel File. To not do this would mean that I tacitly agreed with the evaluation. This I could not allow. My challenge to this evaluation noted the following points:

1. That my Supervisors and co-workers began their campaign of harassment and ostracization immediately after I made the Internal Affairs Bureau aware of the illegal activities of Rocco Barba and the enabling behavior of Police Officers and Police Supervisors. I specifically never used the word "corrupt" because that would have required unquestionable proof of an exchange of money or services in order to ignore criminal behavior. I did not have that proof. I could only note their behavior.

2. I noted that when I called off "sick", I was actually sick and the Sergeant had no proof to the contrary. I was never an abuser of sick time. I had accumulated several hundred hours at that time in my career.

3. The date of the report was in error. It was dated "07/17/78". It was presented to me and signed on 05/17/78,

4. I closed by stating, "The prefabrications in this report and the conduct of supervisors and other officers is an indication of the concerted effort to harass and intimidate me solely because of my efforts to bring to justice a crime figure who makes a mockery of justice. To take me off my sector car that covers the premises of Mr. Barba constitutes a subversion of justice, a breach of authority and is a slap in the face of the citizenry who need and deserve good, honest law enforcement."

Although I submitted this memorandum through channels, I still did not trust the Police Department. I had several trusted friends who worked in the Personnel Department. After several days, I called one of them and asked if my document had been received and placed in my file. This friend indicated that it had been received and included in my file. That gave me a high degree of relief and satisfaction.

I submitted this rebuttal, not only as a means of protecting myself, but also, to eliminate the sphere of deniability among any Supervisor or Commander in my Chain of Command about the activities of Rocco Barba and certain Supervisors and Police Officers in the 5th Police District. I wanted my paper trail to lead to each and every supervisory door. The activity of Rocco Barba and many Police Officers in the 5th Police District had to be stopped or curtailed. I joined the Police Department to be the type of Public Servant I would have been proud to have known in my childhood. If a Police Officer was not going to stop or attempt to stop criminal behavior then who was protecting the community.

MEMORANDUM

o : Police Commissioner (Through Channels)

FROM : Norman A. Carter, Jr., Policeman #5246

SUBJECT: PERFORMANCE REPORT FOR PERMANENT EMPLOYEE

1. I can not allow the abuse of authority which resulted in my receiving three "unsatisfactory" ratings in my last report to pass without comment. The report is full of errors and unsupported assumptions.

2. The date of the report is in error. The report is dated 07/17/78.

3. The "Comments To Employee" section is quite inaccurate. I must preface my statements concerning this section with the following statement.

   a. Since November 22, 1977, when I reported to Staff Inspectors' C and L███ on complicitous indescretions involving certain supervisors, policemen, and a known vice figure, I have become the targe for undue harassment, astracization and life jeopardizing conduct by officers in the 5th District. My health has suffered and it has become necessary for me to take a mild tranquilizer to get through a days work.

   b. The first line of this performance report would lead one to believe that I take off sick whenever given a detail. The record would show that on the numerous occasions I have been detailed out most times I have reported for work. On the occasions I reported off sick, it was because I was sick, and the rater has no concrete reason to believe otherwise.

4. The Third statement concerns incomplete messages on Police Radio, and lack of communication with other officers. If this activity were true, I must question why I was not informed of this earlier by the rater.

   Twice, to my knowledge, it was necessary for complaints to be made to Lt. Ray #209 about my radio broadcasts being interfered with. Many times it was necessary for me to switch to an alternate frequency many times in one day to insure my messages being heard. I was also informed of a conspiracy among other officers not to assist me on assignments requiring more than one officer. This information proved to be accurate. My life, my family's welfare, and the welfare of the public was placed in jeopardy by the very officers that it is alleged my being uncommunicative to. As for my relationship with the public, I am sure that the law abiding public and I get along very well. There may have been complaints filed by a Mr. Rocco Barba of 4326 Main Street. Mr. Barba is a numbers banker, loan shark, stolen goods fence, pimp, and also a good friend of many police and supervisors in the 5th District.

5. My next complaint has to do with the rater, Sgt. Joseph A. Martin, #366. He has not been my immediate supervisor since Nov. 16, 1977. He was cited by me in a report to Staff Inspector's C███ and Lu███ as being too close. an acquaintance of Mr. Barba. I believe in the interest of fairness this invalidates him as a competent rater. On May 17, 1978 at approximately 9:20 P.M., I asked Sgt. M███ to explain his giving me such an unfair rating. His reply was, "The very next thing you do, I am going to take you to the front."

That Police Officers would harass, ridicule, or threaten a Police Officer who was trying to accomplish his sworn duty was an abomination. Sadly, my District Commander and my Divisional Commander were either complicit or incompetent. The 5th Police District was sinking in the quicksand of complicity and corruption. I refused to be pulled down into that putrid pit of infamy in which too many were much too comfortable.

After my Performance Evaluation Rebuttal was submitted, the harassment increased in intensity and frequency. If it rained outside, I would be put on a foot beat in an area where there was neither shelter nor frequent car patrols. I had to either walk or catch public transportation to any foot beat. I soldiered on. Each shift, a Manpower Report would be submitted via computer. Any Operations Team can find out which district may have reported a shortage of personnel due to call offs. Police Districts who required supplemental personnel would normally call other districts to see if they had extra personnel they could use for staffing. This was normally a last resort and was seldom used. My District Operations team would seek out any district reporting a staffing shortage. Even if this meant sending me to an assignment that was on the other side of the city, I would be sent there.

Often, after I arrived for work, they would send me to a district without notifying the district that I was coming. This proved to be frustrating for not only me, but also for the district to which I was sent. Frequently, they would not have an assignment for me. Rather than send me back to my district, the Supervisor would call in a car and have me work with another Officer. I was seldom sent to a district in my own division. Sometimes, it would take me from one hour to two hours to get to my newly designated assignment. It was not only a waste of time. It was a waste of money. My District Supervisors did not care about that. They were concerned only with making my life so miserable that I would either make a serious mistake or resign. I was focused on doing neither. I soldiered on.

In the midst of this, I found out that the Police Internal Affairs Unit had a detail following me whenever I left the district. In addition, I noticed that I was frequently followed home. Because I knew some of the strategies used by surveillance teams, such as have vehicles not only behind you but also driving on parallel streets, I became keenly aware of what was happening.

Once or twice, when I was not in a hurry, I had fun with those who were following me. On the day shift, rather than go directly home, I would take a circuitous route that rambled throughout the north and northwestern sections of the city. I would seek out a parking space near an intersection and park my vehicle. I would not leave my vehicle. I would sit until the easily recognized vehicle would drive past. The surveillance vehicles were normally a four-doored Ford Crown Victoria or a Plymouth Fury. Once the vehicle drove past, I would change my direction of travel. This was the only way I could have some fun with this waste of taxpayer dollars.

I received a tip that there was a great possibility that my home telephone was being monitored. Once I noticed a large Bell Telephone Company utility truck parked for several days outside of my apartment. I never observed the occupants working. Truly, the Department was trying to rid themselves of a nuisance. I directed my informants not to call me at home. I kept my conversations with friends and families brief. Yes, my life was becoming miserable, but not so miserable that I would change my focus. I knew I was correct in what I was doing. Had my supervisors dedicated themselves to providing safety to the citizens of the Manayunk, Roxborough, Wissahickon, and Andorra communities as they dedicated to harassing me, they could have wiped out crime in those areas.

During the summer of 1978, I had one of my most unnerving moments. I must admit that I was more unnerved after the event than I was during its evolvement.

My squad was about to end a midnight to eight in the morning shift. This was a mid-week day. The normal time for my squad's end of shift was 7:45am. At approximately 7:15am, we received an unusual assignment via Police Radio for officers to respond to an auto accident on the Schuylkill Expressway westbound, west of City Avenue. This was unusual for many reasons. Firstly, under normal circumstances a Highway Patrol unit would be dispatched to handle assignments on the Expressway. District personnel would later be called to assist with transporting injured people to hospitals. On this morning, there was no Highway Patrol Unit available. Secondly, the location appeared to be outside of Philadelphia Police jurisdiction.

Nevertheless, a few cars from the 5th District responded. The first unit to arrive reported that a tractor truck with a trailer had left the roadway and had crashed through a concrete wall. The driver appeared to be injured and no one could get to him. Radio Room personnel contacted the Fire Department in order to have a Rescue Unit sent, but there was a concern about jurisdiction. I decided to go to the scene.

There I saw that this was a very bad situation. For some reason the tractor operator had lost control of his vehicle. It had left the road way and crashed through the concrete retaining wall. The two front wheels of cab of the vehicle were suspended in mid-air. Perhaps the weight on the trailer kept the cab from plunging into the Schuylkill River which was about eighty feet below.

By the time of my arrival, no one had spoken to the vehicle's driver. He appeared to be semi-conscious in the cab of the vehicle. I volunteered to climb out to the cab of the vehicle to assess the driver's condition. I obtained a long rope from one of the 5th District EPW's that was on the scene. I tied one end around my waist and asked the officers to hold on to the other end. At that moment I realized that I was entrusting my life to people who did not like me. Still, someone had to try to reach the driver.

I climbed up to the back of the truck. Fortunately, the driver side window was open. The door was locked. This allowed me have something to grab onto as I carefully placed my left foot on the step of the truck. As I looked down, I could see nothing but the dirty brown water of the Schuylkill River. Did I mention that I have a slight fear of heights? I had to lose that distraction and focus on the man in the trunk. I made sure that the rope around my waist was still tight. Thank goodness for my Boy Scout training. I knew how to tie a good knot. I prayed that no one on the other end would let go of the rope.

The driver was semi-conscious. I could not tell whether he had hit his head or had suffered a stroke or heart attack. What was certain was that he could not remain in the truck cab. By this time, an Emergency Response team from Lower Merion Township arrived. Together, we were able to safely remove the driver from the cab. He was taken to a nearby hospital. The next day, an Accident Investigator told me was that the only thing the man could remember was seeing a black face waking him and trying to get him out of the truck.

I was thankful that the man was safely recovering from the accident. I was thankful that I did not slip on that step and have to rely on a 5th

District Police Officer's holding tightly to that rope. All involved survived. Now, my working conditions would return to the chaotic normalcy I had come to expect.

After enduring several additional months of oppressive behavior, I prepared another memorandum to be delivered to the Internal Affairs Bureau. I knew this would result in another interview. This nonsense had to stop. My memorandum was several pages thick. It included memoranda I had written to answer picayune allegations from the despicable Sergeant Spence who made it his mission to persecute me. This documentation looked like a small booklet. Again, I had to use circuitous routes to insure that the memorandum reached its intended recipients.

I had a valued friend hand carry the memorandum to the Police Administration Building. The Police Officer assigned to the Lobby Desk allowed my trusted friend to drop off the memorandum in the Office of the Chief Inspector and the Office of the Police Commissioner. I had everything timed so that the Commanding Officer Northwest Police Division; the Chief Inspector Patrol Bureau North; and the Mayor of the City of Philadelphia would receive the memorandum at the same time. This would anger lower tiered commanders who would be called and asked, "Did you receive this memo? Did you do anything about it?" I wanted chaos. I wanted commanders to squirm.

This was similar to an action I took with a friend while we were stationed at Fort Carson, Colorado. He had submitted a transfer request to attend a special training school. Several weeks passed and he had not received any response in regards to its status. One afternoon, he discovered that this transfer request was buried at the bottom of the First Sergeant's "in box." That transfer had sat unsigned and ignored for several weeks. The friend, whose name was A. Jenkins, and I sat down one evening and drafted a letter. We sent that letter with a copy of the transfer request to our Post Commander, Jenkin's United States Senator and Congressman, the Army Chief of Staff, and to the President of the United States. That mailing caused chaos. The First Sergeant was eventually demoted. Within a week, Jenkins received a late afternoon phone call from a high Army Official. That official told him to pack his gear and to be ready to take a military flight the next morning. We accomplished our mission. That was when I learned there was a lot of power in a well-placed and well written letter.

A day after I had submitted my memorandum to everyone in my Police Department's Chain of Command, I filled out a transfer request. The Juvenile Aid Division was looking to increase its staff. I applied for a transfer to that unit. As soon as my Captain received the transfer, he beckoned me to his office. He was outraged that I would put words in the transfer about how I was treated by him and the Officers of this Police District. I was beyond being impressed by his red-faced outrage. I, politely told him, "Sir, you don't want me to be here. This transfer works for both of us. You will get rid of me, and I will have an assignment I can enjoy." Yes, I was angry, but it was controlled anger. Uncontrolled anger would give the department a chance to come after me and bury the corrupt behavior I was trying to expose. My District Commander (Captain) told me that he would not approve of the transfer, but would forward it through channels. A few days later, I received a phone call from the Commanding Officer of the Juvenile Aid Division. I was instructed to come in for an interview and for a typing test. I interviewed with a Lieutenant. I felt pretty confident after I left the interview. Two days later, I received a call from the Commanding Officer of the Juvenile Aid Division. In short, he disapproved my request. He believed I was more interested in running away from something rather than being truly interested in the job of being an investigator in his unit. He was partially correct. Still, I could have done a credible job in this unit.

On the Saturday following my submission of the memorandum and my transfer request, I was working the day shift. After Roll Call, my actual Platoon Sergeant, Sergeant Waleski, asked me to remain in the building. Both he and Lieutenant Clemens walked me to the Captain's outer office and closed the door. The Captain and his staff were not working. My two most immediate supervisors began a very strange and awkward conversation with me. Their conversation with me began with, "We want to know your problem with this district and the Officers?" They were not loud, but the tone was confrontational. I knew they had been directed to have this conversation by the Captain. I told them that I was not trying to be their adversary. I related that every legitimate action I took against Rocco Barba from parking tickets to abandoned vehicles to reports about his criminal activity had been interfered with by Police Officers. I told them that I felt that I was being set-up by Sergeant Val Spence by having a worker for Rocco Barba attempt to bribe me for my silence.

Both stated that I was overly imaginative. Next, I told Lieutenant Clemens that I heard him when he called me a "creep" as I walked past him in the Operations Room a month earlier. He offered a weak denial, but both of us knew that he said it. Then, I added the following: "When you go home at night and sit around the dinner table with your family do you tell them about how you treat me? Do you laugh about the names you call me? Do you tell them that I am trying to arrest the leader of a burglary ring but you do the best you can to prevent me from doing that? Are you proud of the way you treat me?" Neither answered the question.

Sergeant Waleski made the following statement: "It seems as though you want to change the world all by yourself. You can't change the world." My indignant reply was, "I'm not trying to change the world." What I refuse to do is allow the Department to change me. You cannot tell me, in good conscience, that I am doing something wrong." Neither appeared to understand what I was saying. I was becoming a little irritated. They began to close the conversation. I added that I wanted to make another point. "You guys have fun calling me names, giving me bad assignments, and allowing me to respond to hazardous calls alone. You expect me to come to work smiling each day and tolerate whatever you throw at me. Did you ever think that one day I might come to work angry and go into a rage because of the way you treat me?" The meeting ended with a promise that I would be treated better. Very soon, I would find that this was untrue.

Sick Leave Violation

A few weeks prior to this conversation, I was not feeling well. The weather outside was true Philadelphia winter weather. There were several inches of snow on the ground. I called off for my shift due to illness. Almost every day that I went to work, my stomach would tighten up as I walked into the 5th Police District Building. Some days the discomfort would begin as soon as I dressed to go to work. At one point, I was out of work for nearly two weeks. Several tests by doctors could not reveal why I was experiencing vomiting and diarrhea continually during that period. The final opinion was that I was experiencing some type of stress that was causing my discomfort.

This was one of those times. It was an established policy that whenever one called off sick, one was subject to a "Sick Check". When a Police Officer calls off sick, he must call his Police District each time he/she leaves their residence. The only reasons one could leave one's residence was to see a physician or to go to a pharmacy. My squad was working the day shift. I was off work for the last two days of my shift. My next scheduled shift was the 12am – 8am Last Out Shift.

As was normal for me, I arrived to work about thirty minutes before the beginning of my shift. This gave me an opportunity to go to my locker room before anyone in my squad would be there. This would give me about twenty minutes to sit in the Roll Call Room and read over the previous days' Part One Sheets. As always, I would sit alone in a corner. I felt that if I paid attention to what I was reading, I would not have to look at the rolling eyes of Police Officers to whom I had become a pariah. On this particular night, I could see Sergeant Waleski walk across the Roll Call Room to where I was seated. He was carrying a pink slip with him. He told me that a 35th District Sergeant had come to my apartment building for a Sick Check. As was the departmental policy, the Sergeant filled out an Incident Report (Form 75-48). The pink slip in the Sergeant's hand was the bottom copy of that report. The 35th District Sergeant stated that he came to my apartment building and rang my apartment bell, but no one answered or "buzzed him in." The Sergeant stated that he believed the bells were not operating properly and he left the building. I told Sergeant Waleski that very often the bells were out of order. I assured him that I had been home the entirety of my time off. There was no reason for me to have left my apartment. Sergeant Hawkins stated that he understood and that he felt there would not be a problem.

Almost two weeks later, while working the 4pm – 12pm shift, Lieutenant Clemens called me aside after everyone had left the Roll Call Room. He had a large manila envelope from which he pulled a packet of papers. It contained disciplinary papers known as "Form 75-18". I was almost in shock. What could these be about? Had someone fabricated another violation? As the focus of the Lieutenant's eyes alternately switched from my face to the floor, he informed me that I was being charged with violating the Sick Leave Policy by not being at home during a Sick Check. I was speechless as he read from the form.

The form stated that Sergeant Samples of the 35th Police District made a Sick Check at my residence. The Sergeant stated that he rang the bell for my apartment, but no one answered. He added that he waited for someone to exit the building so that he could walk in and come up to my fourth floor apartment. The Sergeant stated that he knocked several times on my apartment door, but no one responded. This was a complete fabrication. I did not mention that my Sergeant had shown me a copy of the report this Sergeant had submitted. I did not want to put Sergeant Waleski (not his real name) in the bad position of being a witness against this miscarriage of authority. It is important to note that Sergeant Samples who made the Sick Check was a close relative of a Police Officer in my district. This Police Officer was among the group who held me in disdain.

I told my Lieutenant that I never left my residence, but those words were met with a shoulder shrug. As was policy, I signed the document which meant that I had received the form. By my contesting the allegation, I knew that I would have another Police Board of Inquiry Hearing. I knew this was part of a plot to charge me with "repeated violations of policy." Such a charge could result in one's dismissal from the department.

About a month passed before I was given the date of my hearing. I am sure that during that period, my Sergeant was worried that I would ask him about the 75-48 that he had shown me in the Roll Call Room. That would not be a good thing for him, and I did not feel it would benefit me significantly. I never mentioned this to him. I was going to work through this. I was not defeated. I prayed to God a lot during this time. I had to pray for resolution and I had to pray for control of my actions. I could not show anger or resentment. I had to come to work every day and do my job to the best of my ability despite all of the obstacles I faced, i.e., ostracization, distrust, and my fear that I might be the next Officer Frank Serpico.

Frank Serpico was a New York Police Officer who was set up by his fellow Officers and shot in the head by an illegal narcotics dealer. He became expendable after several times reporting corrupt activities by Police Officers. He nearly bled to death because his team was slow to call for medical assistance. I felt I was hated that much by scores of Police Officers in the Northwest Police Division. Arriving at the most innocuous of assignments could be part of a set up for me to be shot or seriously injured by a Police Officer or one of Rocco Barba's workers. This was not hyperbole. I believed my Sergeant and Lieutenant had once tried to set me up with a bribe to ignore the activities of Rocco Barba. There were knots in my stomach every day, but I could not give in. I had to work through it. I knew that I was correct in what I was trying to accomplish. Still, I was suspicious of almost everyone in my job sphere, but I soldiered on.

I expressed my concerns to some members of the Guardian Civic League. One of the Executive Board Members suggested that I have a Police Officer whom they trusted to represent me at the Police Board of Inquiry Hearing. This Police Officer worked in the 16th Police District. He had recently received his Law Degree. He was a Caucasian member of my predominantly African-American Guardian Civic League. We had never met, but I spoke with him over the telephone and explained to him the charges I was facing. He agreed to represent me. He refused to accept payment.

The day of my hearing arrived. As always, I made sure my uniform was well-creased and my shoes were spit-polished. I arrived early. One Police Officer, who was the "peer representative" on the board, recognized me because I seemed to be a frequent visitor. He looked at me with a slight grin as he feigned surprise. "You here again?" he whispered. I nodded and smiled back. Within a few minutes of my arrival, I was approached by the lawyer contracted by the Fraternal Order of Police. It is important to note that this is not a "court of record". Therefore, a lawyer was there only to give advice. He was not an advocate. There were several Police Officers waiting for their hearings. The Fraternal Order of Police lawyer eventually made his way over to me. He read the charge against me. He advised me to plead guilty. The penalty for the first offense of a Sick Leave Violation was a ten day suspension. I knew I was not guilty and I was not going to plead guilty. I told the lawyer that the department was trying to amass charges against me so that they could eventually discharge me for "multiple violations". The lawyer appeared to be upset with my refusal to plead guilty. Shortly after the lawyer left, Police Officer Williams from the 16th District arrived dressed in uniform. I recognized him by his name tag. We sat a distance away from the others and awaited my being called into the hearing room.

When my name was called, Police Officer Williams and 35th District Sergeant Samples arose with me. I had seen this Sergeant's original report he had submitted to my district. What would be his testimony? We walked into the room and took seats at different ends of a long table. On the opposite side of the table sat Police Officers of various ranks. Each was allowed to question witnesses. Police Officer Williams presence seemed to surprise everyone. A Police Officer appearing with an advisor must have been a rare occurrence.

After extensive questioning about his reason for being at the hearing, Williams was told that this was not a court of law. The Board Chairman allowed him to remain as my advisor. Sergeant Samples read his prepared statement about how he had conducted this Sick Check. Prior to the hearing I told Police Officer Williams that I did not in any way want to bring Sergeant Waleski's name into this. I did not want to make him an additional victim. I believed that we could manage my defense without it. Of course, I had no clue as to how I was going to manage to extricate myself from the lies of a Police Sergeant.

As the Sergeant was speaking, Police Officer Williams asked me to describe the door of my apartment. I told him that my door was a very plain brown door with my apartment number. After the Sergeant completed his statement, Police Officer Williams asked him if he could describe my apartment door. The Sergeant responded that it was a standard apartment door with my apartment number and a peep hole. Now, it was my turn to testify. I told the Board that I was well aware of the department's Sick Leave Policy and that I did not violate it. I stated that I never left my apartment until I came in for my next tour of duty. Police Officer Williams then asked me to describe the door of my apartment. I emphasized that my apartment door never had a peep hole as the Sergeant had stated. I added that I never heard anyone knock at my door.

Just prior to the end of the hearing, the Commander who led the hearing asked if I had anything to add to my testimony. I stated that I was innocent of the charge of violating the department's sick leave policy. I added that the allegations put forth at this hearing and at my previous hearings were part of a conspiracy to discredit me because I reported to the Internal Affairs Bureau that certain Police Officers and possibly my Commanding Officer were protecting a man who had a criminal enterprise. One could hear the proverbial pin drop in the room. Some heads seemed to be bowed in either embarrassment or disgust as I was dismissed from the hearing.

Several days later, I received a notice that I had been found guilty and that I must immediately begin a ten day suspension without pay. I was crushed. Still, I tried to put the best light on it. I would have ten days of not having to deal with this insanity called the 5th Police District. No rolling eyes; no stomach pains; and no fear of being assassinated by a disgruntled Police Officer.

And The Walls Came Tumbling Down

On the 4th day of my suspension, I received a phone call from the Internal Affairs Bureau. A Staff Inspector informed me that he was calling in reference to the memorandum I had submitted to everyone from the Mayor to my District Commander. He stated that I must come in for an interview. My goodness, here I was relaxing and on suspension and being directed to come in for an interview. Of course, I told him that I would come in. The interview was scheduled for the next afternoon. I had walked this route before. I had no great expectations. This could very well be a trap. The Fraternal Order of Police had always advised Police Officers to never go to Internal Affairs without someone representing you. All were instructed to call the Fraternal Order of Police so that a representative would be there to protect our interest. My case was different. I was not going there as one being accused. I was the accuser. Months earlier, a Fraternal Order of Police Representative told me they could not represent me in a case where I was accusing other Police Officers of wrong doing. There would be a "conflict of interest". I called the Guardian Civic League. I was a member of the Executive Board. The League was not a bargaining unit, but represented the interest of African-American Police Officers. The Vice President of the League agreed to accompany me to the interview.

The Vice President and I entered a dank room in the dank building located at 319 Race St, at about 2:00pm on a Wednesday. As with my prior experience with Staff Inspectors, there were two present and both had yellow legal pads. I brought a folder with several pages of documentation. After the formal introductions, the Staff Inspectors set the tone for this interview. "We are here because of a memorandum Police Officer Norman Carter sent to the Mayor of Philadelphia. Firstly, Officer Carter, why did you send a memorandum directly to the Mayor rather than through channels to the Police Commissioner?" This was an attempt to cite me for violating the Police Chain of Command. I responded that my first complaint was submitted through channels to the Police Commissioner. An investigation had been conducted and my complaint was deemed as "unfounded" or without merit. This latest documentation was not only submitted to every member of my Chain of Command, but also to the Mayor as he was the next in line to receive a complaint that had not been resolved to my satisfaction by the Police Commissioner. After this explanation, their tone became less confrontational.

The Staff Inspector asked, "Okay, how can we help you, today?" Very methodically, I explained the harassment I had been the recipient of since my first complaint. I told them that either someone from their office or my District Commander had notified Police Officers in the 5th District that I had reported questionable activities by Police Officers. I told them that the information that had been leaked to the Police Officers of the 5th District had been embellished far beyond the information I had given to the two previous Staff Inspectors. I provided copies of memoranda I had submitted to answer for bogus complaints of misbehavior. The complaints about not wearing a hat or not saluting were outright stupid. I spoke of the fabricated Sick Leave Violation. Then, I began to present my documentation of the criminal behavior emanating from Rocco Barba's restaurant.

I stated that even though the Internal Affairs Bureau found no criminal activity coming from the aforementioned restaurant I arrested a "Numbers Writer" who worked for Rocco Barba. I told them about the mishandling of my request for a Search Warrant after I had credible information about stolen fur coats being sold in Rocco Barba's restaurant. I told them about how I had been removed from being assigned Radio Patrol Car 57 and assigned to Radio Patrol Car 513 at the far end of the Police District.

I spoke of the nights I was placed on a foot beat to patrol areas in below freezing temperatures. On those nights, I was told that the only time I could be away from my beat was to either take a ten minute break to go to the bathroom or to take a thirty-minute lunch break. No one worked under those conditions. No one else on any shift walked those foot beats. I spoke of how no one backed me on assignments and that many times my radio transmissions were interfered with. Throughout my interview, I referred to a note book I used as a journal. I detailed to them what I had learned about the operation of the 5th Police District's 5 Squad Officers.

1. The 5 Squad Officers worked outside of the parameters established for such teams in other Police Districts.

2. This team spent a significant amount of time soliciting funds for district "sports teams." I noted to them their solicitation at the night club that was burglarized.

3. In most Police Districts, when a Police Officer took a report of a burglary, the report was taken to his Police District, coded by the Operations Team, and forwarded to the Divisional Detective Headquarters for further investigation. In the 5th Police District, this was done differently. In this district, after a Police Officer turned in his burglary report, it was given to the 5 Squad Officers. The 5 Squad Officers would go the burglarized residence or business and interview the complainant. After their interview, the report would either be sent to the Detective Division or rewritten and recoded as a minor incident. The recoding and rewriting was done without the knowledge of the complainant.

4. One of the more serious violations of trust by the 5 Squad Officers was that they used a Police Department mandate to prevent burglaries as a mechanism to facilitate burglaries. Through television advertisements and through Community Meetings, the Philadelphia Police Department encouraged business owners and home owners to notify the Police Department when they would be away from their properties during vacations or other extended absences. The Police Department promised that Police Officers patrolling the areas of their residences would make periodic unscheduled checks of their properties in order to limit the opportunities for burglars to enter the properties. In the 5th Police District, when citizens contacted the district to notify them of extended absences, the 5 Squad Officers would go to the residence rather than a Patrol Officer. While obtaining emergency contact information and information about the length of time the resident would be away from the property, these 5 Squad Officers Police Officers were making mental notes of valuables in the property.

The 5 Squad Officers would give this information not just to the District Operations Team, but also, to Mr. Rocco Barba. Rocco Barba and his team of burglars would take this information and plan a burglary of the residence or business. Remember that there were many Police Officers in the 5th Police District that were either not vigilant about making proper security checks or they were complicit in the nefarious activities of the 5 Squad Officers.

5. When the owners returned home and reported this incursion into their sanctuary to the Police Department, the same 5 Squad Officers were sent to conduct a "further investigation". The main purpose of their "investigation" was to insure that all items reported as stolen had been turned into Rocco Barba and not stashed away for personal use by his team of burglars. My informants all noted that the stolen items were kept in the abandoned stores owned by Rocco Barba on Main Street.

6. Lastly, I reported that after some burglaries, the complainant would receive a phone call to tell him/her that their property could be returned to them for a certain price. The complainant had to promise not to call the Police Department.

After an hour, one Staff Inspector said that he did not want to see anymore documentation. "What do you what us to do?" I stated that I wanted an honest investigation of criminal activity on the part of Rocco Barba and a cessation of the harassment I was receiving from Police Officers and Supervisors. The Staff Inspector stated that they would investigate my allegations and get back to the Mayor, the Police Commissioner and to me with their findings. I was cautioned (as before) not to speak of this interview to anyone. As the meeting was about to end, the Guardian Civic League Vice President interjected, "My concern is about the safety of Officer Carter. I think he should be transferred for his personal safety." One of the Staff Inspectors responded that at this point they were not authorized to make any recommendations for transfer. This consideration would be passed on to the Police Commissioner after the completion of their investigation.

We shook hands and left the office. On my long drive home, I visualized an exponential increase in the harassment I had been receiving. My past experience with Staff Inspectors had shown they were not in my corner. I had learned not to trust them. Their mission was to protect the status quo. I was a small pebble in their tight shoes. I remembered the words Staff Inspector Lassiter uttered to my Captain after my first complaint, "How do we get rid of this mother….."

I arrived home at approximately 4:30pm. At approximately, 5:00pm, my phone rang. "Hello. Is this Officer Norman Carter?" "Yes, it is", I responded to the unfamiliar voice. "This is Captain Bingham. I am calling to welcome you to the 12th Police District. I need you to report for duty at 11pm on Friday." Today was Wednesday. I was almost speechless. How could I be transferred this rapidly after the Staff Inspectors told me that this could not be done? I responded to the Captain that I was in the midst of a ten day suspension. Arrogantly he responded, "I don't care about any suspension. I want you here, on Friday, at 11pm." I responded affirmatively.

I had heard a lot about Captain Bingham. He was known as a tough talking, short on patience leader. Seldom does a Captain call a newly arriving Police Officer. This is usually done by Corporal or Sergeant. I hung up the telephone and sat quietly contemplating what had just happened. This was highly unusual. Very likely, the Staff Inspectors felt the need to make an immediate call to either the Police Commissioner or the Mayor. This is the only way such a transfer could be done that rapidly.

After several minutes, I called the Guardian Civic League's Vice President. He was as surprised as I. I asked him if he would accompany me to the 5th District to retrieve my gear from my locker. At this point, there is no way that I wanted to return to that building alone. I had been betrayed by the Internal Affairs Bureau once and there was no reason for me not to expect more of the same behavior.

We agreed to meet at approximately 11:00am the next day, Thursday. I quickly went to my locker in the basement of the building and removed all my equipment. I walked out with my arms full. My hope was to never to return to this house of horrors. The 5th Police District, where Honor, Integrity, and Service were the exception and not the rule.

Two months after being transferred to the 12th Police District, I received a phone call from my former Operations Room Corporal. He told me that I had a paycheck that had been sitting in the 5th District for two months. He requested that I come in to pick it up. I was surprised.

I was supposed to have been on suspension for that fabricated sick leave violation. Therefore, I never expected a paycheck. That evening I went to the 5th District to pick up the check. Actually, they could have mailed it weeks ago either to my home or to the 12th Police District. This was another adolescent attempt to display their disdain for me. My check was a full pay check. There was no pay missing for the four days I actually served on suspension. This full check was the Police Department's backhanded way of letting me know that they had found substance in my allegations of mistreatment and malfeasance. No one was going to say this to me. No one was going to apologize. It was left for me to make an inference based on this munificent gesture. I went alone to pick up my pay check. As I was leaving the 5th District for the last time, the Corporal turned to me and asked if I would like to make a contribution to the United Fund. This was an attempt get under my skin. I glared back at him and simply said, "No." This was the last time I walked inside of that den of deceit. In Biblical times, I would have been instructed to leave the building and shake the dust off of my shoes as a testimony of their poor treatment. This had been the nastiest of work environments. No one ever should have been treated as poorly as I was treated there. Only time, a very long time, would heal the wounds to my psyche that were inflicted by the Supervisors and Officers of the 5th Police District.

The 12th Police District - A New Beginning

I am sure every Police Department must have a district, precinct, or assignment where "foul ups" are sent. That was the designation (in more profane terminology) bestowed upon the Police Officers of the 12th Police District. Almost every Officer transferred there would be greeted by someone asking, "What did you do to get here?" For as long as I could remember, the 12th District had that ignominious designation. The district was located in the southwestern most section of the Philadelphia. It was a large district, but not quite as large as the 14th Police District I where I had worked years earlier. Between 49th Street and 62nd St., the populace runs from the severely impoverished at 49th Street to the struggling lower middle-class at 62nd Street. West of 62nd street to the western most boundaries, one would find a predominantly middle class populace. The exception on the western end was the Paschall Homes. These were low-income Public Housing low-rise units.

I came to the 12th Police District in December 1979. It was a very troubling time. The 12th Police District was a racial tinderbox. Homes were relatively cheap. African Americans began to move into what were once predominantly Irish and Italian neighborhoods. Many of these people did not take kindly to this invasion of dark Americans. There were frequent racially charged fights. One playground at 58th St. and Kingsessing Avenue was the focus of much tension. A Caucasian gang known as the "Dirty Annies", would often go to this playground to attack African-Americans in and around the playground. In June of 1979, a member of this gang secreted himself on the roof of a factory not far from this playground. He used a .22 caliber rifle in a sniper attack on three African American teenagers who were playing in the street. One of those teenagers, Tracey

Chambers who was 13 years old, died from multiple gunshot wounds. This event became the fulcrum in the closing of Bartram High School and Tilden Middle School a week before the scheduled end of the school term. Yes, I arrived at a troubling time.

When I arrived that Friday night, I was warmly greeted by Lieutenant Abrams. Lieutenant Abrams was the Platoon Commander for 3-Squad. He was a tall, sharp, African American. He immediately, escorted me to a small office that adjoined the Roll Call Room. After welcoming me to the squad, he added, "I don't care what happened in the 5th District. This is a new beginning. No one here is judging you by anything that happened before you came here." On one hand, this was comforting. On the other hand, it was chilling. Whenever, a Police Officer was transferred to another district, Officers from the receiving district would call the prior district to get an idea about whom they are receiving. Based on the way I was treated in the 5th District, I knew that the response would be similar to, "Watch out for this guy. He's a rat. He went to Internal Affairs and told them every cop in the district was taking money. He is, also, a 'letter writer'." The latter comment was based on several editorials I had submitted to each of the three newspapers in Philadelphia, i.e., The Bulletin; The Inquirer; and the Daily News. In addition, I had been mentioned in the African American newspaper known as the Philadelphia Tribune. The Tribune article was about my speaking out about racial tensions within the Fraternal Order of Police and the Philadelphia Police Department.

My first night, I was assigned to EPW 1204. My partner was a very seasoned veteran. He was a bit upset because on this night, his normal partner was given another assignment because of my assignment to the EPW. It was the same policy of not allowing a newly assigned Officer to work alone for a few days. It did not matter that I knew most of the streets. This was part of the familiarization process. As frustrating as it was for the veteran, who had about seventeen or eighteen years on the department, it was equally frustrating for me. Just as if I were a recruit, I was told not to answer the radio. I had to sit silently as we avoided calls that were nearby. Of course, I was questioned about my career. I was reminded that the Police Department only sent their "foul ups" (a euphemism) to the 12th District. It was a punishment tour for all whom the department considered less than desirable. Still, for me, this was a better existence than my daily trauma of working in the 5th Police District. At least, Police Officers in this district spoke to me.

While my Squad Lieutenant seemed like a polished, well-educated leader, my Squad Sergeant was a bit rough around the edges. He reminded me of the gruff and grizzled Sergeants I encountered in the military. The only difference was that he was seldom profane to the point of humiliation. He was blunt. He knew what he was talking about and he demanded that all of us do what we were paid to do, i.e. be responsible Police Officers who could make good decisions. I grew to like and respect him. Sergeant Wilbur Prescott (his actual name) was the best Patrol Sergeant I ever worked with. As a new Officer, I had to go through the trial period of working with partners, walking foot beats, and assignments to details that all newly arriving Officers go through. In addition, I knew that my co-workers were studying my every move. All they knew about me was what they had heard from the 5th Police District. I understood. I did my job the way it should have been done. I gradually earned their trust. I soldiered on.

About a week into my working in the 12th Police District, I received a telephone call at home from the Internal Affairs Bureau. One of the Staff Inspectors who interviewed me in December informed me that they had investigated my complaint and found that it was unsubstantiated. I expected as much. A booklet of documentation seemed not to be enough. I was disturbed but not defeated. I could look to the bright side of things. I was working in a new district among a different set of Police Officers who did not appear to be shackled by corruption. I, actually, looked forward to coming to work each day.

Two months later, I received a call from a cousin who was assigned to the 16th Police District. It was February 6, 1979. Almost sarcastically, he asked, "Norman, what were you doing in that 5th District?" I laughed, and responded that I had left that horrible place and was happy with my new assignment. He asked if I had read the Philadelphia Daily News. I had not. He stated that my former 5th District Police Sergeant had been transferred to his Police District. He stated that Sergeant Val Spence was furious. The Sergeant told him and several others that he was transferred because I had accused him of taking money from a criminal. I had never made that accusation. The Sergeant further stated that I was responsible for not only his transfer, but also for the transfer of two Police Officers who were part of the 5th District's 5 Squad Officers. I was shocked. A Staff Inspector told me that their investigation did not find any instance of wrong doing by any Police Officer or Police Supervisor.

My cousin further stated that Sergeant Spence told him and others that when he had the opportunity he was going to "punch him in the face". The "him" was I. My pulse rate must have increased by thirty beats per minute. Next, my cousin told me that certain Detectives at Northwest Police Division were angry with me. Rocco Barba had been arrested. No one in Northwest Detective Division was aware that Rocco Barba was being investigated by another agency. They were told by someone that I had made an allegation that they were complicit in the furtherance of Rocco Barba's little criminal empire. My cousin (from my father's side of the family) had no prior knowledge of the problems I had endured in the 5th District. All of the aforementioned information came from the Sergeant who was transferred to his district. Lastly, my cousin told me that the arrest of Rocco Barba was covered in the newspapers. He had just read about it in the Philadelphia Daily News.

Immediately, I went to purchase a copy of the Philadelphia Daily News. The bottom of its Front Page had the headline "Manayunk Theft Ring Broken". Rocco Barba was arrested with two other men. The newspaper reported that over $200,000 dollars in stolen items were recovered. According to the Philadelphia Daily News, the Detectives from the Major Investigations Unit executed a Search and Seizure Warrant at Rocco Barba's restaurant. The article stated, "…in the multi-chambered basement they found enough suspected plunder to fill a pair of 2 ½ ton trucks." The article concluded with, "After the raid it was found that every article seized, including 150 pairs of new men's shoes, had all identity tag labels and numbers removed."

This statement about tag labels being removed reminded me of the time I tried to obtain a Search and Seizure Warrant that was denied by the District Attorney. In the Probable Cause section of the warrant application, I indicated that Rocco Barba attempted to sell a fur coat to one of my informants and the identifying labels were on every coat they saw. Later, I learned that Detectives from the Major Investigations Unit executed four Search Warrants on various properties affiliated with Rocco Barba.

According to court documents, four truckloads of items were seized.

These included a gun, fur coats, an air conditioner, televisions, stereo sets, tires, appliances, clothing, jewelry, and other items. Some items had identifying serial numbers removed. In addition, the Detectives found underground passages that led from Rocco Barba's restaurant to two other properties. Those two properties and another property on the other side of Main Street contained large amounts of stolen property.

At this time, Philadelphia had three major newspapers: The Philadelphia Bulletin, The Philadelphia Daily News, and The Philadelphia Inquirer. All of them gave significant coverage of this arrest. My name was never mentioned. That was an accolade I did not require. Seeing this evil come to an end was all the accolade I required. In my heart, I knew that my perseverance had been rewarded. As a Police Officer I realized that every good deed was not rewarded with an award or a public show of appreciation. Rocco Barba knew the truth. The 5 Squad Officers knew the truth. Sergeant Val Spence knew the truth. This was a time when self-satisfaction was enough.

I felt such elation on reading these articles that it is difficult to describe. Two years of frustration had ended. I had accomplished my task. A criminal who victimized hundreds, if not thousands, of citizens living in the 5th Police District had been stopped and arrested. His days of inglorious immunity were over. Yet, my joy was slightly dampened when I found that some Officers escaped punishment. These were Officers, who by my observation, were directly involved in protecting Rocco Barba's criminal activities. They should have been dismissed and jailed. My feeling is that a political decision was made to temper the punishment of these Police Officers in order to stave off adverse publicity. At this time, the Mayor and the Department were under scrutiny by Federal and State agencies for some unsavory practices. The department did not need public exposure on an issue where investigative reporters may have found that a Police Officer had been blocked from exposing this criminal enterprise for almost two years.

After about two years in the 12th District, Lieutenant Abrams asked if I would like to work in the Operations Room. Initially, I balked at the offer. I enjoyed working with the public. I enjoyed the teamwork and camaraderie experienced working with Police Officers who wanted to do a good job every day. Yes, the district was known as an assemblage of misfits. In working there, I found that most of these Police Officers gave their best every day. We had a few bad actors, but there was nothing close to the oppressive obstruction of law and order that I had experienced in the 5th Police District.

Eventually, I acquiesced to my Lieutenant's request and I took on the challenge of working in the Operations Room. I worked with a team lead by a Police Corporal. There were two other Officers who worked in the Operations Room and one Turnkey. The Turnkey managed the small cell block that served as a temporary holding area for prisoners and males who were intoxicated and disorderly. After I became comfortable working in the Operations Room, I made it an opportunity to learn more about how the department worked. I read journals and taught myself how to use several systems on our computer that many who worked in the Operations Room did not know existed. I became the data retrieval expert.

A few weeks after I began working in the Operations Room, a former Supervisor from the 5th Police District came into our Operations Room. At this time he was assigned to a special patrol unit. He came into our building to obtain gas for his Police Vehicle. This Supervisor appeared to be startled when he saw me. I felt the same way when our eyes met. I did not speak to him. He did not speak to me. He treated me rudely when I was assigned to the 5th District. I turned my back and continued with my assigned work. After several uncomfortable minutes, the Officer left the Operations Room. After he left, one of my co-workers, Officer Mike Norris, asked me. "Do you know that guy?" I responded that he had worked with me in the 5th District. Officer Mike Norris went on to say that the Officer stood behind me and stared at me for several minutes while he was in the Operations Room.

About a month later, the same Police Officer came into the Operations Room and the same thing occurred. Officer Mike Norris, again asked, whether there was something wrong with him as he continued to come into the room and stare at me for several minutes while the Turnkey serviced his vehicle. His presence made me uncomfortable, but I did the best I could to ignore him without being rude. This occurred a few more times.

One evening, the Police Officer entered our Operations Room and stood behind me for several minutes. Suddenly, there was a tap on my back. "Excuse me Carter. May I have a word with you in private?" Nervously, I stood and walked with him into the subdued light of the Roll Call Room.

We were alone. Even under the subdued light, I could see that he was abnormally pale. With a shaken voice he began, "Norman, I just want to apologize to you for all that you went through in the 5th. Time has shown that you were right and we were wrong. I am hoping that we can let bygones be bygones and that you will accept my apology." He extended his hand. It was shaking. Internally, I was shaking. This was a man I had grown to dislike for his open rudeness to me. Now, he had the courage to humble himself and ask for my forgiveness. I shook his trembling hand and said the only words I could think to say, "I have moved on. All of that is water under the bridge." "Thank you", he replied. He smiled and left. I returned to my desk. Officer Mike Norris, quickly asked, "What was that all about? I was ready to come out there." I answered, "He wanted to apologize to me." "Apologize for what?' Norris asked. I did not want to go into detail. That would generate too many questions. I replied, "He just wanted to apologize for some things that happened in the 5th District." That was all I wanted to say. I never saw this Officer again.

Sometimes They Come Back

On October 3, 1979, I and hundreds of other Police Officers were given Center City Assignments to provide crowd security for the arrival of Pope Francis. One good thing the Police Department did well was mobilize during exceptional circumstances. During this event, my 12th District Squad was assigned to cover the 300 Block of North Broad Street (between Vine Street and Callowhill Street). We were almost directly across the street from Philadelphia's two largest newspapers, the Philadelphia Inquirer and the Philadelphia Daily News. We were, also, a short distance from the Fraternal of Police Headquarters at Broad and Spring Garden Sts.

During a lunch break, I happened to meet my cousin, Oscar, who was assigned to the 16th Police District. He, also, was assigned to this detail. This was the cousin who told me that my former Sergeant wanted to "punch him in his face". Sgt. Spence was not only angry because he was moved from the 5th Police District and had a much longer ride to work, but also, because he was permanently assigned to the District's Task Force. This meant that his permanent shift was 5pm – 1am on most weekdays. "Task Force" on the District level was a pool of officers from other squads within the district who acted as a supplemental crime patrol. My cousin warned me that Spence was detailed to this event. I had promised myself that if he attacked me, I was not going to resist. If he hit me, I would fall to the ground and not get up. Then, I would sue the Police Department and press criminal charges against this Officer. This seemed to be the only way to retaliate for the mistreatment I had suffered in the 5th Police District.

As my cousin and I were walking south on the east side of Broad Street, I happened to turn my head slightly to my left. My cousin was walking on my left side. Suddenly, I saw this Sergeant walking towards us in a crouched position. He was trying to conceal himself behind parked cars in the 1300 Block of Pearl Street. When I told Oscar that the Sergeant was approaching us, he grabbed me by the back of my blouse coat and began to push me in a southerly direction away from the approaching Sergeant. "No, Norman. Not today. Keep walking", he urged. I was so off balance that I could not stop my feet. The Sergeant ended his dastardly pursuit and I went back to work. I was a bit shaken for several minutes. No one in my squad was aware of what happened. My cousin returned to his assignment after he was sure that I was calm. The Sergeant never spoke any words and I never said anything to him.

A Rocky Criminal History

Many years later, I did some research on Rocco Barba. I found news articles going back to 1947 showing him to have been involved in a series of crimes from 1947 through 1970.

Those articles mentioning Rocco Barba were"

"Two Held for Robbing Oak Lane, Olney Homes" – Phila. Bulletin- Mar. 22, 1947

"Ship Cabin Burglaries Charged to "Salesman" – Phila. Inquirer – Sep. 3, 1952

"Bail Set for 3 suspects in Check Thefts by Gang" - Phila. Inquirer – July 21, 1953

"One Suspect Freed in Money Order Theft" – Phila. Inquirer – July 27, 1953 (The freed suspect was Rocco Barba. "He was with Dillon and Berkery when they were arrested Saturday morning in Barba's apartment."

"DA Gets Warrant for Records of Tours Agency" – Phila. Inquirer – Jan.28, 1970

This meant the Police Department and particularly the Commander and Supervisors of the 5th Police District should have been well aware of his criminal behavior. The Internal Affairs Bureau should have noticed this behavior pattern. Such a behavior pattern would have added credibility to my allegations of criminal behavior. As with other career criminals, his information should have been posted in the 5th Police District. This was not done. Police Officers and Police Supervisors openly fraternized with Rocco Barba. It was against departmental regulations to fraternize with known felons (people who have committed serious crimes).

I had observed one Police Officer who frequently walked out of Rocco Barba's restaurant with items that were not food. A cursory investigation by the Internal Affairs Bureau would have easily revealed this. Instead, an Investigator from Internal Affairs came into the 5th Police District and directed his profane and administrative vitriol towards me. That Investigator purposely sabotaged a legitimate complaint about criminal activity and police complicity. More damning was this complaint was made by me. I was a Police Officer who was not involved in any unsavory or illegal activity. I was doing my job. I was serving my community in the best way that I knew. It was never my goal to seek out bad Police Officers. I only sought to prevent criminal behavior and to arrest those who worked to disrupt a community. In this instance, Police Officers, including the Internal Affairs Bureau, intentionally shielded Rocco Barba. The behavior of the Internal Affairs Bureau was part of the reason Police Officers were and possibly still are reticent to report criminal behavior by other Police Officers. It is the perfect way to maintain an atmosphere of intimidation and retaliation that is uncomfortably similar to behavior exhibited by those involved in organized crime.

They'll Never Ever Learn

The Command Inspections Bureau was composed of Police Captains and Inspectors who worked during the evening hours. Each Captain was assigned to either one or two Police Divisions. They worked the evening shifts between either 6:00pm – 2:00am or 7:00pm – 3:00am. They responded to homicides, serious assaults, bomb threats, large fires, and any other assignments that might require coordination with other city agencies. They were the evening substitutes for the District Commanders who worked during normal business hours. We called them Night Command.

One Night Command Captain was a frequent evening visitor to our district. I worked with him when I was a young Police Officer in the 14th Police District. He was a pleasant face to see. We always greeted each other warmly. He was quick to brag that I had "broken him in" as a rookie Police Officer. During his Probationary Period, he was among a long chain of young recruits placed with me. One evening, Captain McClain (not his real name) called me aside. He was elated because he had received word that he was going to leave Night Command and be assigned to a District. He would become a District Commander. This was a position of high esteem. My dark face must have become ashen as he told me that he would be assigned to the 5th Police District. I tried to smile as I congratulated him. In a few minutes, he was back on patrol. As I sat back into my office chair, I found myself in a quandary. Here was a guy I liked. He was about to take command of that cesspool known as the 5th Police District. Should I warn him or keep quiet?

A day later, Captain McClain stopped into the 12th District's Operations Room. As he left, I walked behind him. Before he left the building and away from other Officers, I told him to be watchful. I told him that, normally, I do not like to talk about my stint in the 5th Police District, but I felt he needed to be aware of the problems that I knew existed in that District. I did not mention the names of any Police Officers or criminals. I just told there were several Officers of questionable character in his new assignment. He needed to be watchful. He thanked me for the warning. That was my last time seeing him in person. The next time I saw him, was a few years later on a television news program.

In 1984, this Captain, five other Police Commanders (including a Deputy Police Commissioner), and one 5th District "5 Squad" Police Officer were found guilty of extorting over $350,000 in bribes from gambling operators. It broke my heart to see this Captain, whom I had warned about corruption in the 5th Police District, embarking on a shameful trek towards prison. I knew him as a decent and dedicated Police Professional. He lost his career, his sizable pension, and contact with his family. Being the subject of negative news coverage on television, radio, and the print media is devastating to not only the Police Officer, but also his family.

This was a tragedy that should never have happened. Year after year Police Officers with good careers have fallen prey to the easy from the sleazy. With dirty money, you could pay the mortgage on a home you could not normally afford; or bought an expensive car; or sent your children to an expensive private school; or bought a summer home along the New Jersey Shore. You obtained all or some of the aforementioned luxuries, but there was one thing you could not obtain. You could not obtain true peace of mind. Corrupt Police Officers impressed me as people who believed their network of thievery and deceit was invincible. These Officers never understand that the people who smilingly give them money or services for ignoring illegal activity will use them as insurance against long jail sentences if they are ever arrested. These Police Officers become bargaining chips in the judicial world of plea bargaining. Is your good standing in the community worth that? Is dragging your family through your dirt worth that? Is tarnishing the reputation of every Police Officer who comes to work to do a good job worth that? The answer should always be a resounding and emphatic "No". Unfortunately, the temptation of easy money from sleazy criminals is too much to resist for many.

One afternoon, while working in the 12th District's Operation Room, a Lieutenant who worked in an undercover status in the Southwest Police

Division called. I answered the telephone. This Lieutenant asked to speak to a Lieutenant from a squad other than mine. As it was time for shift change, the District Lieutenant came into our Operations Room. I gave him the message and a phone number to call. He stood next to me while making the call. After the call ended, the Lieutenant began a rant of outrage. "Do you know that guy told me that there was an opening for a Lieutenant in his unit?" The Lieutenant said that when he told the caller that he might be interested, the caller tried to entice him by saying, "Come on down. The water's fine." This was code terminology that illegal payoffs were significant. The Lieutenant refused the offer. A few months later, the Lieutenant who called and several Police Officers in his unit were fired and arrested for taking bribes to ignore illegal activity. Some never learned. Some will never learn. No matter the rank, so many have sank into that tar pit of graft and disgrace.

The Road to Hell

Although, I was somewhat reluctant to leave working on the street, I began to embrace and enjoy working in the Operations Room. I began to learn a lot about staffing, policies, and procedures. I was still uncomfortable with the way some crimes were downgraded. Some felonies became either misdemeanors or minor incidents. All stolen vehicle tags became lost tags. There remained that insipid "Try and Locate" list. This list was problematic to me not only because it was grammatically incorrect (It should have read "Try to Locate"), but also because most of the vehicles on this list were actually stolen vehicles that were several years old when reported stolen. This is the same situation I complained about to my Supervisors when I was a recruit in the 14th Police District. This was a city-wide policy that adversely affected people living in either low or middle income neighborhoods. I still complained about it, but nothing changed. This was an ingrained and systemic failure in the Police Department's Crime Reporting system. It was a disservice to the entire community. I vowed to keep fighting to resolve this issue, but I continued to be a small voice in a very large and resistant crowd. I remained emotionally wounded from my experiences in the 5th Police District. I was not ready to champion that particular cause at that particular time.

While working in the Operations Room, I decided to learn as much as I could. I was not quickly embraced by my co-workers in the Operations Room. When my Lieutenant asked me to work in the Operations Room, he stated that he had a suspicion that some things might be going awry in the Operations Room when he was not around. He wanted someone in the Operations Room that he could trust. He clearly stated that he did not want a "rat" in there, but he wanted someone with character who was strong enough not to allow wrong doing to occur without interceding. One thing I learned in later years was that Operations Room teams were usually composed of close friends. I was the outsider. Remember, everyone knew that I had come out of the 5th District with a reputation for not tolerating bad behavior in the workplace. I ignored the expected chill and concerned myself with learning as much as I could as fast as I could. During lulls in activity, I would read instructional manuals about our computer system. On the overnight shift, when work began to slow down after 3:00am, I studied those manuals and related Police Directives. One member of the Operations Team who taught me a few things was promoted to Police Corporal. I saw that as an attainable goal for me.

Still, there were challenges. Some Officers were a bit too physically forceful when handling prisoners brought into the District. Most of those brought into the District were brought in for Public Intoxication or minor summary offenses. Some Officers believed in verbally abusing people when there was no need for it. There were times when I interceded and discretely asked the Officer to calm down or I tried to expedite the processing of the person. It was obvious, that I was not going to tolerate someone being beaten. There was one African-American Officer who frequently brought in intoxicated males. He would put them through a rapid battery of questions, then he would become angry if their responses were slow. I pulled him aside after one such incident. The conversation was similar to this:

Me: "Listen CJ, why did you bring this person in?"

CJ: "Because he's drunk."

Me: "Okay, if he is drunk then that means he is not going to be as sharp as you.

He's drunk, right?"

CJ: "You're right."

Me: "Okay, then why are you looking for an intelligent conversation from him or any other drunk. Just get their name, age, and address. Put them back in a cell. Don't make an incident out of nothing."

CJ: "You're right, Carter. I won't let it happen again."

Actually, it never happened again. No one else knew about our conversation. Others noticed a change in his behavior. I never commented about it. I wish I could have had that same cooperation when I was in the 5th District.

The Highway Patrol Saga

Sometime around 1986, the Police Department decided it needed to crack down on intoxicated vehicle operators. The Department placed this responsibility on the Highway Patrol Division. Most of this unit's Officers did not patrol the two main highways in Philadelphia. They were used as a supplemental crime fighting force in certain Police Districts. The Highway Patrol Division devised an incentive program in order to increase the number of arrests for intoxicated vehicle operators. If a Highway Patrol Officer arrested a person for operating a vehicle while intoxicated, he would be granted a half-day off with pay.

First, I must bore you with the process. Whenever a Police Officer arrested a person for operating a vehicle while intoxicated, he had to bring the offender into the Operations Room of the District of occurrence. The Operations Supervisor (usually a Police Corporal) was responsible for visually insuring that the person arrested appeared to be intoxicated. This had to be visual because we did not have equipment to test anyone's blood or breath. Normally, this visual inspection was a cursory check. Police Corporals, normally, trusted the judgement of the Police Officers in their squad.

What I began to notice was that all of the Highway Patrol Teams (two Officers per car), were arresting middle-aged men leaving a tavern at 56th St. and Chester Ave. Most of these men had never been arrested before. All were African-American. Most did not appear to be intoxicated. Because my Corporal trusted the Officers, he seldom made a close appraisal of the offenders brought into our Operations Room by the Highway Patrol Officers. My suspicions peaked when an arrested man protested that he had only been in the tavern a few minutes. He stated that he went in to purchase a six-pack of beer. He strongly protested that he never had a drink while in the tavern. He was on his way home to drink beer with his wife. The man was near tears. I will never forget the look of desperation in that man's eyes.

The next day, I had a private conversation with my Corporal. I pointed out to him the number of arrests the Highway Patrol Officers were making at or near 56th St. and Chester Ave. I told him that my suspicion was that the Highway Patrol Officers were sitting outside of this tavern and waiting for anyone to exit and get into a vehicle. Once the person drove away, they arrested him and falsely charged him with being intoxicated. I told the Corporal that these Officers were more concerned about getting an extra day off than they were about making a quality arrest. I told him this type of behavior would eventually backfire on these Officers. Almost all of those arrested would pass a Breathalyzer Test which was an examination given to all persons arrested for this type of offense. This examination tested the level of alcohol in a person's system. It was administered after the arrest at the Police Administration Building. Minimally, this was a waste of time for the Police Officer who administered the Breathalyzer Tests. Maximally, this was an incursion on the civil rights of every person these Officers arrested. My feeling was that when a number of these arrests were invalidated after the examinations, some Police Official or Lawyer was going to inquire about which Corporal approved these arrests. There would be a very unsavory investigation with dire consequences for the Corporal who signed the paperwork for the arrests. My Corporal agreed with me.

That very night, another Highway Patrol Team came in with an arrest for "Intoxicated Chauffer" (the actual name for this offense). The alleged offender was brought in from 56th and Chester Ave. The Corporal intensely inspected the male who was brought in. In a direct manner, he told the Police Officers that this male was not intoxicated. An argument began. My Corporal never had a problem speaking his mind. After several minutes of pointed conversation, the Corporal responded, "I'm the Corporal. I made the determination of whether or not this man is intoxicated. In my view, he is not intoxicated and you must release him unless you have another charge on him."

The Highway Patrol Officers were extremely angry. They stormed out of the District. They left the man they had arrested. We never had another

Highway Patrol Officer bring someone into our Operations Room while our squad was working. This incident was passed on to all squads in the 12th District. To my knowledge all stopped accepting these bogus arrests. This was how you change bad behavior. You don't have to go to Staff Inspectors or Internal Affairs. You can handle things on your level as long as you have a supportive team. We had that in the 12th Police District. I was proud of my team.

Going to School

After about three years in the Operations Room, I was asked if I would like to work inside of a Junior High School. The Police Officer assigned to Shaw Jr. High School at 53rd and Springfield Sts., was about to take another assignment. Because, I had more seniority than many in the district, I was given first option for this assignment. I had never thought about working inside of a school. It was one of the choice assignments that I thought would never be offered to me. It was a day shift job with all weekends and holidays off. I had slightly less than seventeen years on the job and this might be a great assignment to end my career. Still, it took me a couple of days before I agreed to take on this new challenge. Soon, I would learn that this job was not a "piece of cake". This job was labor intensive.

My first day working at the school was truly a day to remember. I arrived at approximately 8:00am. I reported to the Main Office and met the Principal. He introduced me to his office staff. Afterwards, I began to learn the names of this large school's teachers. The job seemed easy enough until the end of the day. In the midst of a crowd of about twenty students I saw two girls of about eleven years of age fighting. These girls had their hands firmly locked on each other's hair as they struggled like miniature sumo wrestlers. I had a very difficult time trying to remove their hands from each other's hair while not trying to injure either girl. This took several minutes. This would be the first of scores of fights that required my intercession. Fights are what children do. What was more alarming was the vermin who preyed on the young girls who attended this school.

During the lunch period when the children were allowed to play in the schoolyard, young men from fifteen years to twenty-four years of age would come into the schoolyard and attempt to talk to the girls. Eventually, I put a stop to that by finding two sets of chains to lock the two gates of entry into the schoolyard. I still had to closely monitor the gates in the event an emergency arose which would require me to open them. The problem with older boys and young men coming to entice eleven to fifteen year old girls to leave the school was a perpetual problem. Once I began to arrest these trespassers, the problem abated slightly. Still, many of them would wait until the end of school. They would try to stand on corners near the school, but I would ask them to move. If they failed to heed my warning, I arrested them for disorderly conduct. No one was looking out for these young children.

Worsening the problem was a drug dealer I will call Mike. Mike lived a few houses away from the school in the 5300 block of Springfield St. Several parents had warned me about him. He liked to talk to these young girls. He was nearly thirty years old. I confronted him several times about loitering near the school. He would leave, but would eventually find a way to return on another day.

I noticed that Mike frequently talked to a uniformed Police Officer who was assigned to this sector. Not only would I see Mike talking to this Officer, but several times Mike would get into the front seat of this Officer's Patrol car. This was highly unusual. They would drive off to an unknown location. This was a problem. It reminded me of scenarios I encountered in the infamous 5th Police District.

One afternoon, this Officer, who had never spoken to me parked his vehicle on 53rd Street outside of the schoolyard. He beckoned me to come over to his vehicle. When I arrived, he introduced himself, then began to politely chastise me for "harassing" his friend Mike. I told him that Mike had no business loitering around the school and talking to the young children. I added that I did not allow Mike or any other non-student to loiter around the school. His response was to tell me about how nice of a guy Mike was. Now, he was arousing my indignation. I stopped being polite. I told him that I knew that Mike was a drug dealer and that I did not want him talking to these children. I added that I had seen him driving Mike to unknown locations and bringing him back home. There was a department policy that dealt with unauthorized persons in Police Vehicles. I told him that if Mike continued to loiter around the school and engage in conversations with these children that I would arrest him. The Officer appeared surprised at my indignation but he remained adamant in his defense of his friend, Mike.

I told the officer that if he was going to be Mike's protector, then he might suffer the same fate as Mike. The Officer drove off as if he were at the starting line of the Indianapolis 500. He never spoke to me again. Mike stayed away from the school. About two years later this Officer was fired from the Police Department. He stood Roll Call with a white power visible on his dark mustache. His Supervisor ordered him to have an examination for use of an illegal narcotic. The Physician employed by the City of Philadelphia found that this Officer had cocaine in his system. He was immediately terminated.

A more distasteful practice quickly ended after my intercession. One afternoon at approximately 1:15pm, a man of about forty years of age walked through the Front Entrance of the school. I happened to be standing there with a Non-Teaching Assistant. The fashionably dressed man was accompanied by two girls of about fifteen years of age. He spoke to the Non-Teaching Assistant (NTA) who was seated at a desk and stated that he had a family emergency and was coming to pick up his niece. The NTA recognized him as having been to the school before to pick up this particular student. The NTA was about to give permission for the male to go up to the Office. I suspected that something was not in order. I asked the male for his name and told him that I would go the school office to ask for the young girl, who was about fourteen years of age to meet him.

Instead, I went to the office and told a worker what had occurred. The worker knew the "uncle" as he had been there before. I asked for the Emergency Contact for the child. The worker gave to me the phone number for the child's mother. I called the mother at her place of employment. I told her that her daughter's uncle was at the school to pick her up due to a family emergency. The mother's voice rose two octaves. There was no family emergency. In addition, she stated the child did not have an uncle with the name given by the male. The alarmed mother asked me to not release her daughter from school until the normal time. She was going to leave work and meet her daughter at the normal end of school time.

By the time, I returned to the Front Entrance the male and the two girls with him were gone. The next day, the mother came to the school with her daughter. We met in the School Principal's Office. There we found out that this male had picked up her fourteen year old daughter several times on the pretense of being her uncle. No one at the school had checked to see if the male was an emergency contact. The mother had no idea about these early dismissals. Further information revealed that this male was a pimp who used young girls as part of his stable of prostitutes. The mother stated that she would have a further conversation with her daughter to determine if she should pursue criminal charges. I gave her the phone number for the Sex Crimes Unit. I believe she removed the child from the school. I never saw the pimp again. These instances demonstrated the hazards children faced after they were in school.

After almost three years of assignment at Shaw Junior High School (which became Shaw Middle School), I took a promotional examination for the position of Police Corporal. I passed the examination and I was promoted in February 1988. After my promotion, I was assigned to the 3rd Police District in South Philadelphia. This was no small accomplishment. When I criticized a mayoral candidate, who happened to be the former Police Commissioner, I was threatened by the then current Police Commissioner with not ever receiving a promotion. I had waded through the muck and mire of the 5th Police District and survived. I had overcome a lot and now with twenty years of career behind me, I finally realized a promotion. I was going to make the best of the remainder of my career.

The Third Police District

Because of my training in the 12th Police District's Operation's Room, I was confident that I could supervise an Operations Room. Firstly, the workload in the 3rd Police District was about half of what it was in the 12th District. A Corporal in another squad was the person who gave me my initial training when I began working in the 12th District's Operations Room. I knew that I could use him as a resource if I ever ran into a problem. During the first few days as the Operations Room Leader, there was palpable uneasiness. Everyone was extremely friendly......overly friendly. One of the Sergeants (there were two), worked in the 12th District while I was there. My Lieutenant was my Sergeant for a short period, twenty years before in the 14th Police District. The District Captain, had a reputation of being a tough-talking, no nonsense, task master. As a Corporal, I knew that I might have a lot of interaction with the Captain. His office was adjacent to the Operations Room.

The 3rd Police District was one of four Districts that comprised the South Police Division. The South Police Division was the testing ground for a pilot project in the Police Department. Every squad in every District in the Division, had a civilian Operations Room Clerk assigned. The idea was to make more Officers available for patrol duties rather than working in an Operations Room. This was an unexpected challenge. I had a young African American female whom I shall call Bess. Bess was about twenty-two years old and I felt that this was her first significant job. Just as all of us, she was required to work swing shifts. At the time of my arrival, she was doing the same job that I had done when I first began working in the 12th District's Operations Room. That job was to separate, file, and distribute vehicle and pedestrian investigations and to type certain reports. When I had that assignment, I would complete my initial work as soon as possible and look for other tasks to take on. I noticed that Bess would complete her initial work and she did very little after that. I candidly suggested to all that Bess take other assignments in the event someone called off due to illness or went on vacation.

The two Police Officers assigned to the Operations Room told me that this was not the policy. They told me that Bess could only do the menial task she had been doing for about a month. I found this to be an extreme waste of a resource. There was no way I was going to have an Operations Room where someone was restricted just because they were a civilian. At this point, I just absorbed information and pondered it. I did not want to make waves at the beginning of my tenure. I knew there would be a proper time to address this issue. Now was not the time.

It only took about a month before I had to deal with my first crisis. A Police Officer turned in a Burglary Report. A business had been broken into during the night. There was evidence of forcible entry, but the complainant stated that nothing was missing. The normal process was that Police Officers would turn all reports into the "48 Man". The "48 Man" was the Operations Room Assistant who was responsible for coding all reports. In addition, this Police Officer insured that the Corporal was made aware of all serious offenses. In addition, this Officer forwarded reports of serious crimes to the South Detective Division. After the Patrol Officer gave the "48 Man" the report, he read it, and then told me that he was going to code it as a "Criminal Trespass" rather than a Burglary. The reason for doing this was that a Burglary was a Part One Crime. Part One Crimes were serious offenses that required an investigation by a Detective. Part One Crimes were totaled and reported to the Federal Bureau of Investigation at the end of the year for their Uniform Crimes Report. Departmentally, there was pressure to keep the number of unsolved Part One Crimes to a minimum. Police Captains, Police Inspectors, Police Commissioners, and Mayors were graded on how well they controlled crime. It did not matter whether you suppressed crime with additional Police Officers (added fiscal cost) or with an "eraser". The "eraser" was used frequently within the Police Department. I protested that when I was a rookie Police Officer and throughout my career. Now, my ideals were being tested. I was in charge. I was responsible. I asked the Police Officer who was my "75-48 Man",

"…what happens if the complainant calls back tonight and reports that he found something missing?" "I'll leave a note for the person coming in after me and I will submit the report the Officer gave me." I told him this was not acceptable. We were not going to start falsifying incidents. He responded that this was the way it was always done. He happened to forget that I had worked for almost five years in an Operations Room. There was little he could tell me that I did not know about policies, procedures, and "going down with crimes". I insisted that he properly code the report and submit it to Detectives. He said that he would, but what he actually did aroused my ire. He went to the Sergeant that I knew and told him about it.

Once the Sergeant, who years before had been a "75-48 man" confronted me, I politely told him that I was not going to have my name placed on a report that I knew was false. It was my responsibility. I was willing to take any heat that came from above. He shrugged his shoulders and said, "You're the boss in there, Norm. Whatever you want." I was steaming. This was not going to be the way my Operations Room was going to be run. I needed to head this off before it became worse.

The next morning, I asked to speak with the Captain. I knew he could be quite gruff, but this was important. About 10:00am, his Secretary told me that the Captain was ready to see me. Once there, I told him about the entire incident. In short, I told him that I was not comfortable with changing crime reports. I was surprised when he responded that I was "in charge of your Operations Room and you run it the way you see fit." He was not at all interested in fabricating reports. He wanted to know exactly what was going on in his district. I was almost breathless, but I was not finished. I told the Captain that no one ever clearly explained to me the duties of the Civilian Operations Room Assistant (CORA). I mentioned that I had been told their duties were restricted to light typing and filing Pedestrian and Vehicle Investigations. The Captain related that this was never the case. He stated that the Civilian was supposed to learn every task related to working in the Operations Room, including coding Police Reports, notifying Detectives of serious offenses, and any other duties except handling prisoners.

I felt, I had a new lease on life. He closed by stating that if I encountered any problems to come directly to him. I assured him that I did not think that would be necessary. The last thing I wanted to do was to be running into the Captain's Office whenever I had a problem. He had given me my marching orders. I had a clear vision of my mission. I knew what it was like to work in a smoothly run Operations Room. This was not the case in the 3rd Police District. Some toes were going to be stepped on. This was actually "My Operations Room."

The next day, I told my staff that I wanted Bess to learn everyone's job. This meant that she would have to shadow each of my two Operations Room Police Officers. They openly balked. I told them that this was not their choice, but was the way I wanted my Operations Room to function. Our conversations were not loud, but my authority was being challenged. Once I convinced them that I was unmoved in this mission, they appeared to reluctantly accept my directive. I was forcing them to work against an established behavioral norm. They failed to appreciate the fact that civilians were going to be an integral part of every Operations Room. I told my staff that I had come from a District that was much busier than this one. I added that if they did not wish to accept this new direction, they were free to return to street patrol. I told them that I was capable of running this Operations Room alone rather than have the dissension I was experiencing.

The Police Department, as a whole, was always resistant to change. What I was experiencing in my Operations Room was a microcosm of the Department's mentality of holding on to old practices, even when those practices worked to your detriment. This was why, despite a national trend to the contrary, the Philadelphia Police Department was among the last large Police Departments to allow women to work uniformed patrol. It was why the Philadelphia Police Department, silently, kept a quota for hiring and promoting non-Caucasian Police Officers.

The Mini-Revolt

On certain days of the week, my District was the location of Preliminary Hearings for all misdemeanor and some felony arrests for the South Police Division. This was a function of, at least, one Police District in every Police Division. It was a labor intensive day for the Operations Room Team, as we not only had to complete our normal tasks, but also monitor and secure prisoners who may have not been able to post bail prior to the hearing. On this particular day, one of my Operations Team had previously requested and was granted a day off. My thinking was that we could operate with one less person. On the day of the hearing, my other Police Officer called off sick. This left me with a civilian ORA who did not have a clue about how to work at any of the other positions. In actuality, I was working alone. A Police Officer in my squad related to me that this was done on purpose as a show of discontent with the new direction I was forcing them to accept. My "48 Man" was on his way to visit a good friend who was a Supervisor at the Police Administration Building. He was seeking to transfer out of the district because of the stand I was taking.

It became an expectantly busy day. The end result was that every required task was done and done timely. I began to train Bess on working the "48 Desk". What the angry Police Officers did not know was they had sealed their fate. My "75-48 Man" soon obtained his transfer. I, immediately, moved Bess to his position. This aroused some eyebrows in my squad and my district. I did not care. No one could justify her not working in that position. All of this occurred because some Police Officers were stuck on the stupid and immoral practice of downgrading crime reports. Now, I was confident that I had someone in the "48 Man" position whom I could properly train and trust. Bess became an extremely competent Operations Room Assistant. She not only remained in that position throughout my remaining tenure in the 3rd Police District, she went on to become a Police Officer and as of 2014 was a Police Sergeant in the 17th Police District.

My argument with the Fraternal Order of Police and with the Philadelphia Police Department concerning their tacit support of the falsification of crime statics was this:

1. As an organization, assumed to have earned public trust, why were we falsifying crime reports?
2. When you lower crime statics in high crime areas:
    a. You give the public a false sense of security.
    b. The Mayor and the Police Commissioner become justified in reducing the number of Police Officers on patrol. The Fraternal Order of Police should have been championing a responsible staffing level for Patrol Officers.
    c. With reduced staffing, justified by lower crime statistics, Police Officers on patrol are at greater risk of not having sufficient support when they encounter hostile situations.
    d. Situations that might be easily controlled by sufficient back up Officers may degrade to the point that a Police Officer may have to resort to deadly force to prevent serious injury or death to himself or others.

Under Mayor Frank L. Rizzo (former Police Commissioner), who served as Mayor of Philadelphia from 1972 until 1980, the Police Department employed approximately 8,300 Police Officers. In 2016, this department is currently staffed with approximately 6,600 Police Officers. Some pseudo-erudite political leaders managed to convince a misinformed citizenry that they were using Police Officers more efficiently. That became the façade they used to reduce staffing and present to the public financial records showing how well they were managing the city's budget. With smiling faces, Police Commissioners, Mayors, and City Managing Directors stood proudly while scores of families became victims of murders, rapes, burglaries, and major thefts. There will always be crime. The scores of families of which I speak were those whose victimization was a direct result of the anemic staffing of Police Officers. While Police Officers cannot prevent all crime, you must admit that lessening the number of committed law enforcement professionals leaves the public at a greater risk for increased crime. All of this was justified by falsified crimes reports. How this practice existed for decades without one person having the moral backbone to complain about it was/is beyond my understanding. This practice made a joke of the Philadelphia Police Department's motto of "Honor, Integrity, and Service".

The Narcotics Field Unit

By 1990, I had become comfortable and confident in my position as Operations Room Supervisor in the 3rd Police District. I acquired a great deal of experience, not only in established policies and practices, but also leadership. My entire team was composed of a civilian and three Police Officers who had a clear idea of my vision and who took pride in their job.

Almost from the beginning of my promotion to Police Corporal, a friend of mine, who was a Police Officer in the Narcotics Field Unit continually asked me to apply for a transfer to the Narcotics Field Unit. In late 1983, this unit was rocked by a corruptions scandal. Police Officers in that unit were accused of stealing money from drug dealers. It was a lucrative assignment for corrupt cops. I wanted no part of it. I rejected every invitation to join that unit until I received a call from a Police Corporal whom I knew from my relationship with the Guardian Civic League.

He called me because the Department was going through a reorganization. Because of this reorganization, there would be a surplus of thirteen Police Corporals. It was decided that certain Corporals could be placed in the Narcotics Field Unit as a supplement to the Sergeants in each squad. This would give each squad more flexibility and free the Lieutenants to do administrative work. Our conversation took place while I was at my work desk. I could only see this as my walking into quicksand. I had a good job that I was enjoying. At this time in my life, working in an undercover unit that had been plagued with scandal over many years was not something I was seeking. After about fifteen minutes, he put the Inspector on the telephone. I knew and respected this Inspector. He was known for his integrity. I had met him, also, through my affiliation with the Guardian Civic League. We were not friends. I just knew him.

The Inspector began by stating that he would like for me to be a part of his unit. Seeking to stop the conversation short, because no Commander wants a problem worker, I stated, "Inspector, I am sure that you know my reputation. There are a lot of things that I will not tolerate. I don't want to cause conflict in your unit." His reply startled me. "Norman, I know all about your reputation. That is why I want to have you in my unit. I need people I can trust." Wow!! Someone wanted me because I was uncompromising when it came to my intolerance for corruption. He went on to say that the Narcotics Field Unit wanted to move past the previous scandal in which Police Officers were arrested, convicted, and sentenced to prison terms. I began to re-think my resistance to join the unit. The Inspector sounded sincere. I trusted him. I decided to join the team. In two weeks, I was going through my orientation as a Corporal in the Narcotics Field Unit.

My first assignment was to work with the team that covered the Central Police Division. This Division was comprised of the relatively small 6th and 9th Police Districts which protected the Center City and Fairmount neighborhoods of Philadelphia. It appeared as though I was assigned to a good team. Working in civilian clothes was new to me. I came to work in clean and pressed business casual clothes. I was working with Police Officers wearing tattered blue jeans and wrinkled khaki pants. I would need to make a clothing adjustment. Almost everyone looked overdue for an appointment with a shaving razor. I never understood why the first thing Police Officers working undercover thought to do was to grow a beard. Later, after being ridiculed for looking like a school teacher, I decided to join the crowd. I never could cultivate a heavy beard. It took weeks to attain a relatively small growth of facial hair.

On our first big arrest for narcotics trafficking, I found that all was not as rosy as I had come to believe. Dirty money sticks to the hands of greedy cops. It was amazing how they had so much trouble getting this dirty green stuff off of their hands.

The area we worked had a large Hispanic population that was gradually being gentrified in the northwestern portion of the Division. Ironically, the northern area west of Broad Street and north of Spring Garden Street had served as my paper route when I was a young teenager. As a child, this was an area populated by predominantly Puerto Rican, Irish, and Ukrainian immigrants who were aggressively pursuing the American Dream. As a Paper Delivery Boy, I was always amazed by the fact that many families who could barely speak English would take daily delivery of the Philadelphia Inquirer. This was their way of immersing themselves in the English language so that they could better the lives of their families. Now, this area had been taken over by users and sellers of illegal narcotics. During both portions of my experiences in this neighborhood, it was extremely helpful that I was fluent in the Spanish language. I had a rudimentary understanding of the Russian and German languages thanks to the early teaching of these languages at Roberts Vaux Junior High School.

On this particular day we executed a Search and Seizure Warrant in the northeastern portion of the 6th Police District. We arrested several people for possession and sales of narcotics. In addition, we seized slightly less than $3,000 in bills of denominations no larger that $20.00. As after all arrests, we re-assembled at our divisional headquarters to process the arrests. This was my first experience processing an arrest this large. The Sergeant and I had a small office adjoining the larger room used by the five Police Officers in our unit. A Police Officer brought all of the money into our office and closed the door. He counted the money while I did other paperwork. After several minutes he gave the money to me and asked me to count it. He left the room. My count agreed with his. He returned to the office several minutes later. When I told him my count agreed with his, he asked me to count it again and left the office. I found this strange. Again, my count remained the same. He returned to the office. I told him that my count remained the same. He replied, "This still does not sound right to me. Please count it again." He left. I was steaming. I knew this game. I had heard about it before. He expected me to take out a portion of the money for him and me. My hands began to shake and I broke out in a sweat. This could not be happening to me. This could not be happening in the Narcotics Field Unit that had been rocked by scandal recently. Was this Officer this dumb and this greedy? I tried to calm myself down by the time he returned to the office. I sternly told him that the count never changed. He appeared to be nervous and frustrated at the same time. He placed the money on a property receipt and placed it in a plastic bag so that it could be processed and delivered to the Evidence Custodian. Now, I knew I had to watch this guy. We worked in this tiny little office and I had to watch him. A blow up was destined to happen.

Late one afternoon, we made a street arrest of a male and a female who were selling crack-cocaine on the corner of 11th & Poplar Sts. This was the northern edge of the Richard Allen Housing Project. It was an easy "buy and bust". This meant that one of our Officers purchased crack-cocaine with marked money and we immediately made an arrest. We confiscated crack-cocaine, money, and a large portable radio/cassette tape player. Everything was processed normally and all evidence was taken to the Evidence Custodian except for the large portable radio/cassette tape player. It had been properly placed on a Property Receipt and should have been taken to the Evidence Custodian. One Officer stated he wanted to hold it as "evidence". I kept my questions to myself. The audio unit remained in our headquarters for over a week. The Officer indicated that the radio could be better secured at his home. I lost my temper.

I asked, why was this considered evidence? It should have been returned to the owner. We should never have kept it this long in our office. Almost the entire team was in the office. As was normal, I am relatively soft-spoken. All were surprised. I was not trying to be loud, but I was not trying to whisper. Eventually, the reluctant Officer disposed of it properly. Any question I had about the integrity of this Officer had been answered. Not only was he a potential thief, but he was setting a dangerous tone for our unit. I was not going to tolerate it. The worse that could happen was that I would be removed from the unit and transferred to a Police District. This would not be a problem for me. I worked in this Division for about four months.

Because of a vacancy, I was transferred to the Northwest Division of the Narcotics Field Unit. This unit was Heaven sent. The Sergeant and I developed an immediate rapport. We had the same goals and the same ideals. The Police Officers were professional and hard working. They challenged each other and assisted each other. Everyone wanted to do a good job. As a result, we were able to take down two large narcotics operations in two housing projects in the Northwest Division. Because of the danger, most Police Officers refused to enter Housing Projects because all had "lookouts" who would notify their network of any suspicious person or vehicle that entered their area. Our team took them on and we were very successful. In addition, while I was away on vacation, the team made a significant arrest for heroin sales in the 5th Police District. This had never been done before. The 5th District was always ignored. I was proud of my team.

Around February 1992, I began to think about retirement. I was forty-six years old. As a rookie Police Officer, I promised myself that if I did not attain the rank of Captain by the time I was forty-five years old that I would retire. I had overstayed my internal visa by one year. My thinking was that after a certain age, you have to face the fact that your reflexes are not as sharp as they were when you were younger. Any Police Officer over 45 years of age who was working in the streets was placing himself in danger. It was a reality check that was often dismissed by Police Officers because of economics and testosterone. The correctness of my decision would become clear to me in late April of 1992.

After several narcotics purchases and extensive surveillance, we executed a Search Warrant on a property located on Atlantic Street in the northwestern section of the city. Unfortunately, our surveillance and purchases never revealed that the front door was reinforced in order to impede forced entry. First we knocked and announced ourselves. No one answered the door, but we knew that people and a large amount of crack-cocaine were in the property. Several Officers went to the rear of the property to watch for anyone trying to escape via the rear alley. We began to use a battering ram on the door after no one answered our knocking and the announcement that we were Police Officers. It took several tense and exhausting minutes before we were able to breach the door. I was the first person to enter the door. Less than eight feet away a man was pointing a rifle directly at me. Even though I had my pistol drawn, I did not shoot him. I ran directly up to him, grabbed the barrel of the rifle and pointed it to the ceiling. The guy was frozen in his position. I had to hit him in the face with my left hand before he released his grip on the rifle. This was dangerous. It was nearly fool hearty. I was not trying to be a hero. I just did not think to shoot. That was a case of slowed reflexes. That could have been a fatal mistake. A week later, I chased a young drug dealer about six city blocks on foot. When other officers and I captured him, I was totally exhausted. Years before, I could run several blocks and not feel this exhausted. I was becoming too old to do this job. Yes, it was time to think about retiring. I retired in June of 1992. Everyone knew how much I loved my job. I was happy with my team. All thought that I would stay away for a few months and return. They had no idea of my resolve. I did not realize that the Police Department and I would have interactions years into the future.

The Poisoned Romance

In the fall of 1984 a childhood acquaintance, who was a Police Officer, played matchmaker and introduced me to a young lady. She was attractive, intelligent, and gainfully employed as a nurse. Over a period of months, our relationship (on my part), became one of exclusivity. After a few months, a behavior pattern that would be repeated over a span of thirteen years evolved. Our romance would be intense and dependable for a few months, then she would vanish. I knew this was a character flaw, but I cared about her enough to tolerate it. In 1991, this woman joined the Police Department. Still, the same behavior pattern persisted. On approximately, November 16, 1997, my tolerance had reached its terminus. She began to absent herself from the relationship, not by words, but by actions. My phone calls and beeper alerts were not answered. I realized that at fifty-two years old, I was hamstringing my future by investing my time, sincerity, and love in someone who was unappreciative and capricious. During that time, I was very active and athletic. Her being nine years my junior did not seem to be a factor. She was just not capable of maintaining a substantive continuous relationship. She could be continual, but never continuous. That was not enough.

Around November 18, 1997, she came to visit me at my home. As usual, I was alone at home. For several years, she had a key to my residence. We had a very calm and intelligent conversation about the status of our relationship. She wanted "a little space" for a short time. I told her that I had been so tolerant of her behavior pattern over the years that asking to have "a little space" seemed insulting. Our conversation continued calmly. I told her that this time around, she could not depend on me to be waiting for her when or if she decided to return. I told her that I needed someone in my life who could be committed to a substantive relationship. We embraced and gave each other a parting kiss. I felt no anger. I felt no resentment. We had entered into an amicable agreement that seemed to be satisfying to both of us. I thought that if a relationship ended, this was the way it should happen. There was no screaming and no profanity. Two adults had reached a point in their lives where moving in a new direction was mutually realized.

Over the next few days, she began to call my residence. She would always ask if I was doing okay. After the third or fourth day, I told her that she no longer had to call me. I was doing fine and she should focus on doing well for herself. The phone calls persisted. I refused to answer my phone when I saw her name appear on the "caller identification" display on my telephone. The calls came during the evening and during the middle of the night. They became very annoying. After almost a week of these calls, I took my telephone receiver off the cradle to keep it from ringing. Unfortunately, because I had a messaging module as part of my telephone package, all unanswered calls immediately went to the messaging module. This lasted for several days. At this time, I was working as a Supervisor for the Philadelphia Office of Pennsylvania's Office of Inspector General.

This woman, whom I will call Myrna, eventually began to leave messages on my home telephone to vent her frustration about my not answering my telephone. Venting was fine, although the behavior seemed to be incongruent with the desire she had expressed on ending our relationship. She would get over it, I thought.

Beginning on the evening of November 25, 1997, a despicable saga of meanness and revenge began. Myrna was Police Officer assigned to a non-uniformed unit. She, also, was a woman scorned. Myrna left two threatening messages on my telephone's answering system during the evening. The messages were left because I refused to answer my telephone. In both messages, Myrna threatened to "serve me with some papers." I had no idea of what "papers" she was serving me. We did not have children. We were not married. This evening, a female friend arrived at my home at about 8:00pm. We had been friends for several years. Both of us were horror movie fans. We decided that this would be a good evening to pig out on junk food and watch a few good horror movies. This was just before

Thanksgiving Day. I would be off from my job at the Inspector General's Office until the following Monday.

At 3:00am, November 26, 1997, my doorbell rang. My first thought was that this had to be my former girlfriend. My door opened to two grim faced Police Officers from the 35th Police District. After I admitted them inside, they announced that they were advising me that Myrna had taken out a Protection Order against me. They told me that I was to keep away from her and that I had to appear before a Judge.

According to them, Myrna stated I had come to her residence that evening and threatened her. All of these allegations were absurd prevarications sworn to by a Philadelphia Police Officer. I had been home almost all day except for a brief period when I went to the store to get a copy of the Philadelphia Daily News. I had submitted to the Daily News a "Letters to the Editor" opinion and it was printed that day. I began to plead my innocence of the allegations to the Officers, but that was an exercise in futility. What was odd was that since Myrna and I were not living together, there were no exigent circumstances that required them to come to my home at 3:00am. This violation of procedures was done purely because Myrna was a Police Officer. It was mean spirited. It was wrong. It was devastating. My guest decided to stay until the morning. Until she left, I could not talk about anything except this fabricated Protection Order that required me to appear before a Judge to answer the allegations. This incident was recorded of Police Incident Report 97-35-1123XX. This latter fact is important.

Both my guest and I were shaken by this event. She knew that she had been with me at my home during the time that Myrna stated I was at her residence. The Police Officers could clearly see that both of us were watching television in my Living Room. Early the following week, I went to a Domestic Relations Courtroom in downtown Philadelphia. I had secured an attorney via my benefits program with the Fraternal Order of Police. My attorney convinced me to not protest the Protection Order but to enter into a mutual agreement that we would stay away and not contact one another. At the time, that appeared to be a rational solution that would keep her from calling me. I agreed to his suggestion. It was so ordered by the Judge. I went home satisfied, but still puzzled as to why Myrna would take such an action against someone who had never harmed her.

On December 15, 1997, Myrna contacted me several times at my office via telephone. Each time I answered the telephone, the call would rapidly degrade into Myrna engaging in a profane tirade that had no basis in reality. Each time, I abruptly ended the call by hanging up the telephone. I was very concerned. Myrna seemed to be mentally unhinged. I called my telephone's messaging system to find that Myrna had left a veiled threat. She stated, "Yeah, I have a key." There were no other words said, but I knew this was becoming a much more serious matter than I had expected.

Remember the "Agreement Without Admission" order from the Court prohibited her from contacting me or coming to my residence. I left my job immediately after hearing this message. After arriving home, I called for a Locksmith to come that afternoon to change my door lock. Still, erring on the side of caution, I wanted to have the preceding events documented in case something more serious would occur. I decided to file a Police Report. Because my complaint was against a Police Officer, a Police Sergeant came to my residence. The Sergeant arrived. I recognized him as having been in the same Police Academy Class as Myrna. I informed him of the events leading up to my call. I played for him the message left by Myrna. Without my prodding, the Sergeant admitted that he was a good friend of Myrna and that he could not imagine her ever behaving in this manner. He left my residence with me feeling as if I was the bad guy. His responding to my call was recorded on Police Report 97-35-1187XX. Once he left, I knew that I had to take this a bit further than a Police Sergeant whose professional judgement was clouded by friendship with the accused.

I sincerely believed that Myrna had become mentally unhinged. I decided that I needed to take my concern beyond this simple report. I went to the Police Internal Affairs Bureau early that evening. I hated walking into that building. I had been there twice as a complainant and both times I found this unit deficient. That was several years ago, maybe it had changed. As I walked into the building, I saw a friendly and familiar face. Sergeant Delso (not his real name) was sitting at the reception/intake desk. When I was a Corporal in the 3rd Police District, he was a Police Officer in the 4th Police District. Both Districts were located in the same building. After a friendly exchange, I told him my reason for being there. As with any private citizen, I had to fill out a complaint form. As I was filling out the form, I remembered that he should have known Myrna as she had worked in the 4th Police District prior to her assignment to the non-uniformed unit. I was sure this did not matter.

Because I of my prior experiences with the Internal Affairs Bureau, I wanted to remove as much doubt as possible about the veracity of my complaint. In addition to submitting the form I was filling out, I gave to Sergeant Delso a tape with the recorded messages Myrna had placed on my telephone's answering module. The investigation was assigned Internal Affairs Complaint Number 97-XX8 and Police Report Number 97-35-1187XX. He told me that an Investigator would contact me in the near future. At that time, I would have to return to be interviewed. I did not relish returning to this building, but I knew I had to do whatever it took to stop the madness.

When I returned home that night, I placed a video camera near a window that focused on an area immediately outside of my home. Because each video tape would last only two hours, I had to constantly get out of bed and change the video tape. The next morning, I reviewed the video tapes from that night. The very first tape showed that Myrna parked her car outside of my home at 11:18pm. Once I viewed the tape, I checked my front door. There were scratches all over the brass face plate of my new lock. This showed that she had tried to enter my home while I was asleep. Here was a crazed Police Officer who was aware of a Court document that prohibited her from contacting me, trying to enter my home while I was asleep. Had someone told her that I had filed a complaint against her? This was a repeat of behavior that occurred when I filed a complaint with Internal Affairs while I was a Police Officer in the 5th Police District. I did not realize at the time that Myrna's worked with someone with supervisory authority who not only worked with me in the 5th Police District, but also was once assigned to the Internal Affairs Bureau. This convoluted escapade into corporate malfeasance was not only ponderous, it was also ridiculous. The pompous purveyors of deceit risked their careers in order to teach me a lesson. The lesson was that if you expose bad cops, we will find a way to make your life miserable. The suppression of the truth is more important that our careers and our families. We don't care how long it takes, we will get to you.

On December 18, 1997, I went to the District Attorney's Office to file a complaint because of terroristic threats and harassment. Myrna's actions indicated that she was taking overt actions to harm or harass me. In filing my complaint, I informed Detective Reynolds (not the real name) that I had audio and video evidence to back up my complaint. I mentioned that her coming to my home was immediately after I had filed a complaint with the Internal Affairs Bureau. Days later, I received a notice in the mail that my complaint lacked merit. This was becoming frustrating.

On December 31, 1997, I went to the Internal Affairs Bureau to be interviewed by Lieutenant Mahoney (not her real name). I gave her a formal statement of all that had occurred during and since the night that Myrna filed her perjured sworn complaint against me. Lieutenant Mahoney told me that she had listened to the audio tape. She stated that there was no way to tell when the tape had been recorded and that there was no assurance that the person on the tape was Myrna. I told her that each message on the tape was date and time stamped. She shook her head indicating that this was not the case. I could not believe that this was occurring. Either the Lieutenant was lying or someone had altered the tape I had given to Sergeant Delso.

Because I expected a little stonewalling from the Internal Affairs Bureau, I pulled from my attaché case another copy of the taped messages which included the date and time stamp. The most important message was the last which said, "Yeah, I have a key." I could see a grimace on the Lieutenant's face. She sighed in disgust. Before she could say another word, I presented to her a copy of the video tape of Myrna's coming to my residence on the same evening I had filed a complaint. Now, I knew there remained untrustworthy people assigned to the Internal Affairs Bureau. If they would sabotage evidence from a retired Police Officer, what chance does an average citizen have when they file a legitimate complaint against a Police Officer?

On January 1, 1998 at about 4:56am, my home telephone rang. I looked at the LED caller identification display on my telephone. I did not recognize the phone number. I did not answer the telephone. After several minutes, I listened to the message. It was from Myrna. She stated, "You f….. up. You really f….. up. Now you'll have to live with this." This was my confirmation that for the fourth time in my experiences with the Internal Affairs Bureau, some had been immediately informed that I had made a statement about them.

I activated "call trace" through the automated function on my telephone service. That morning, I wrote and mailed a letter to Lieutenant Mahoney concerning this phone call. On January 9, I called her to confirm her receipt of the letter. She stated that she had received it. I told her that I had activated "call trace" for this call and that she had my permission to retrieve the information from Bell Atlantic's Call Center. I, also, told her that I had recorded the message I had received.

On May 19, 1998, Lieutenant Mahoney called me via telephone and informed me that my complaint against Myrna was not substantiated. She had closed the investigation. She stated that if would like to review her report, I was welcome to come into the Bureau. I told her that I would like to review the report. She gave me a date to come in when she was working. She warned me not to bring any cameras or recording devices with me. In addition, I could not take notes. This was stupid. I am the complainant and I cannot receive a copy of the report nor can I take notes.

On the day that I went in to review the report, the person at the Intake Desk directed me to a Conference Room. The door was open. When I looked inside, my eyes must have looked as though they were burning with fire. There were five or six Police Officers laughing and joking. Among them was Lieutenant Mahoney and former Police Officer, now Sergeant Sanger. Sergeant Sanger was a member of the infamous 5th Police District 5 Squad Officers I had mentioned in my complaint to the Internal Affairs Bureau several years prior. Because of my second complaint to Internal Affairs, he had been transferred out of the 5th District. He was now assigned to the Internal Affairs Bureau and worked with Lieutenant Mahoney. This was insanity. Lieutenant Mahoney directed me to a nearby small room to read her investigation. I could still hear their laughter as the door to this had to remain open. Supposedly, she could not find any evidence to corroborate my complaint. She falsely put in her report that my audio tape was not date stamped. She added that my video tape was inconclusive. (To this very day, I have the original copies of the audio and video tapes with their date and time stamps.) What was most unsettling was that she closed her investigation on March 26, 1998. She did not notify me until May 19, 1998. By this delay, my compliant was placed outside of the timely submission policy of the Police Advisory Commission for an appeal of the finding. Lieutenant Mahoney knew that and her boss knew that. This was a conspiracy of silence designed to frustrate me and emasculate my complaint. I had trusted them to do a credible investigation. My summation was this:

1. An Officer in Myrna's Major Crimes Unit was a Police Officer in my squad in the 5th Police District. In addition, he had spent time working in the Internal Affairs Bureau.
2. Very likely, the mishandling of my complaint (including the erasures on the 1st audio tape submitted) was a corporate payback for my interrupting a criminal enterprise in the 5th Police District. Over 15 years after I had left this district, ill feelings persisted. Misguided and mean spirited Police Officers were willing to risk their careers by approving what they knew was a bogus investigation.
3. Lt. Mahoney never mentioned the "call trace" information. I, had even taken to her a copy of my phone bill which indicated the trace of the phone call. Obviously, she sabotaged this investigation.

After giving myself a few days to think, I called a Police Official in the Internal Affairs Bureau whom I knew personally. We had worked together several years before. We both knew each other very well. I explained to him the events that had occurred with Myrna and with Lieutenant Mahoney. I will never forget his words. He took a deep breath and said, "Look Norman, we know the bitch is lying but there is nothing I can do about it. I hope you understand what I am saying." He added that he trusted that I would never mention that he had said these words to me. It was clear to me what this Police Official meant. There was directed internal pressure to sabotage my complaint. It was retaliation that had been approved by Command Level directives. There was nothing someone within the department could do to resolve this miscarriage of authority.

Although, I continued to send letters to Police Commissioner John Timoney, Mayor Ed Rendell, District Attorney Lynne Abraham, and Chief Public Defender Ellen Greenlee I never mentioned this conversation. I was looked upon as a nuisance by all of the aforementioned. I wanted them all, especially the Police Officials, to be continually reminded about their wrongness and their callousness. In my letters, I even detailed the connection between my exploits in the 5th Police District, and how that may have influenced the Internal Affairs Bureau. They were using Myrna as a tool for their revenge. Supposedly, they were teaching me a lesson about speaking out against the status quo. They did not know they were stoking a fire within me. I was not one who gave up when faced with administrative inertia. They knew how adamant I was in pursing the arrest of Rocco Barba. Even experiencing almost two years of harassment did not keep me from finding a way to expose criminal behavior and departmental lethargy. Now, that I was retired, did they think I had less resolve? They grossly underestimated me.

A Manager from my job at the Office of the Inspector General advised me that because I was taking to task the District Attorney's Office for nonfeasance I was going to cause a conflict of interest. The Office of Inspector General was a politically sensitive department. We had to work closely with the District Attorney's Office. Without seeking further advice on the matter, I resigned my position as a Claims Investigation Supervisor. It was not a financially sound decision. It was a decision I made to prevent any encumbrance on my quest to undo a wrong that I felt damaged my character. I had a great job, but the unbridled pursuit to stop an injustice was more important to me.

Rather than sit and stew in the juice of my emotions, I allowed myself a release through exercise. Prior to our break up, Myrna and I took morning jogs at various locations in the northern sections of the city. Eventually, we settled on jogging at LaSalle University's Athletic Field which was about a mile from my home. The university allowed members of the community to use the facility when it was not being used by students. For about a month we jogged together at this field. Shortly thereafter, cold weather set in and we stopped using the field. Before warmer weather returned, we were no longer seeing each other. Keep in mind this field was about three miles from her residence.

Beginning in early March, I returned to jogging at the field. At the time, I did not have a car. I walked to the field each morning between 5:00am and 5:30am. My normal workout for the day consisted of a combined walk-run of four to five miles. On April 21, 1998, I noticed three police patrol cars and one emergency patrol wagon near the entrance of the field. My thought was they were conversing about some event that recently occurred. As I continued my workout, vehicles gradually began to leave. One remained. I completed my workout and was leaving the field when the remaining Officer hailed me. "Are you Norman Carter", he asked? I replied in the affirmative. He went on to relate that a female Police Officer named Myrna wanted me arrested for violating a "restraining order." There was no "restraining order". The earlier one had expired. This was not only bizarre in my mind, it was bizarre in the Officer's mind. I never saw her at or near the field. I had not seen her in months. Obviously, I was being stalked in the early morning hours by a woman whose behavior had become not only vindictive but irrational. This' event was recorded on Police Report 98-35-398XX. I am chronicling these events because, as I mentioned earlier, if the Police Department was playing such tricks on me, the average citizen had a very slim chance of achieving redress through the Internal Affairs Bureau.

Because I wanted to save every document concerning the bizarre behavior of Myrna, I called the 35th Police District to obtain the District Complaint number for the report about this latest incident. The Operations Room Assistant first stated that there was no report of an incident at that date and time. I thought that perhaps I had given her the wrong date for the event. I ended the call and checked my Physical Fitness Chart to obtain the correct date and time. I found that I have given the 35th District Officer the correct time. The next day, I called again. I spoke to the same Officer. I gave to her the exact time, date, and the name of the Police Officer who spoke to me. After checking, she stated that she still could not find on the Report Transmittal Sheets for that date or in the 75-48 file a report of any incident at LaSalle University's Field. I knew this could not be true. I had seen the Police Officer write his report. I had given to him my name. There had to be a report. Further conversation with this Officer was not going to be productive. Perhaps this officer was in the same squad as Myrna's friend, the Sergeant who had come to my house.

Because of my familiarity with how Police Incident Reports are processed, I waited a week and then called the Police Department's Reports and Control Unit. That action revealed that a report was made and it contained all of the information I wanted. The 35th District Operations Room Assistant had lied to me twice. I was able to obtain the report number. As was policy, I followed the proper procedure for obtaining a copy of Incident Report 98-35-398XX.

After this event, my family became very concerned. Other than a morning run and an afternoon walk of about three miles, I isolated myself at home. I kept a video camera trained on the front of my property at all times. It ran almost all day every day for a year. This stopped when the camera burned out and I could not afford to replace it. I kept my equilibrium by bible reading and listening to music. I thought I was doing well until I shared some of what had been happening to me with one of my cousins. She stated, "You must have done something to make her act this way. I think there is more to the story." She was one hundred percent wrong. But her statement made me wonder if other friends and family members were thinking the same way.

Now, I shared with no one any of the continuing events with this female Police Officer who was on a mission to destroy my character. She thought she had the Police Department in her back pocket. Actually, the department was using her. She was doing the dirty work that pleased them. For me this meant more prayer, more music, and more resolve not to let this series of events wreck my sensibilities.

The Beginning of the End for
Statistical Manipulations

B y the summer of 1998, I had lost any respect I had for the leadership of
the Philadelphia Police Department. I had been dealing with months
of lies and deceit. In early July 1998, a highly ranked Police Official spoke
at a predominantly African-American Community Meeting near to my
neighborhood. At that meeting several community members complained
about the rise of crime in their neighborhood. The Police Official's response
aroused an anger within me that had been simmering for years. He told the
meeting's attendees that crime was actually declining in this neighborhood
and throughout the city. He stated that the "perception of crime" was
driving the fears of the community rather than actual crime. His remarks
were printed in the news media. This was a horrible statement to make
from a man who should have been more sensitive to the anguish these
people were living under. It had been several months since I had made a
submission to the "Letters to The Editor" sections of either the Philadelphia
Daily News or the Philadelphia Inquirer. Now it was the time, again. I was
not going to allow the department to hide behind another lie.

My submission to the Philadelphia Daily News was brief and to the
point. I stated that the Police Commissioner's statement about "perception
of crime" was not true. I mentioned that manipulating crime statistics was
a pattern of behavior that had existed for years. I added that if the readers
wanted substantiation of my allegation, all they had to do was to look at
the crime reports and try to find reports of stolen motor vehicle license tags.
I told the readers they would find none because the Police Department
routinely made all stolen tags "lost tags".

Weeks passed and I forgot about this "Letter to the Editor" until I received a telephone call from Philadelphia Inquirer Staff Writer Mark Fazlollah. He was elated that someone with personal knowledge of how the internal mechanism of the Police Department worked had submitted such a letter. He had been working on this topic for some time and my letter provided him with substantive information for a pending investigative article. I was bubbling over with excitement. Someone was listening to me. This might be the beginning of a change in crime reporting that I had been seeking since I was a rookie Police Officer thirty years prior.

A few weeks later, I received a phone call from a Producer for the Dateline NBC television program. Recently, there had been some truly distasteful misreporting of crime events by the Philadelphia Police Department. Recent crime victims, one in Center City and one from the Kensington section of the city, found police reports from incidents in which they were involved were either missing or altered. In one incident a shooting was reported. In another incident a man was severely beaten. Each incident was downgraded to either "unfounded" or "minor disturbance". These discrepancies were reported in the newspapers and on televised news programs. Now, there was a new Police Commissioner. He was an outsider from New York. His name was John Timoney. He decided that he did not trust the crime statistics that were submitted to him. He ordered an audit. In November, I was interviewed by Hoda Kotbe (currently a cohost for the NBC network's "Today" show) for a Dateline NBC segment entitled "Playing the Numbers".

Someone was listening. Not just the city of Philadelphia but the entire country would know about this abysmal practice of the Philadelphia Police Department. Citizens had been hurt and placed in danger and the Police Department decided it was more important to sweep these events under their blue rug of deceit rather that search for the offenders and make the public aware of the dangerous people freely walking in their communities. My interview lasted for about three hours. Only about two minutes of my interview appeared on the program which was televised on January 13, 1999.

By the time the program was televised, Police Commissioner Timoney submitted a revised crime statistics report (nationally known as the Uniform Crime Statistics Report) for the year 1998. Overall, there was a nine percent increase in crime. More alarmingly, there was a large increase in violent crimes:

a.   Rapes were up 14.9% over 1997
b.   Aggravated Assaults were up 44.7% over 1997
c.   Thefts were up 20.6% over 1997

Police Commissioner Timoney's reaction to this falsification of Police Reports was not to dismiss the Commanders who turned in these reports (as departmental policy called for), but to transfer them and allow them to keep their ranks and pay. If one reads between the lines, they were not dismissed because what they had done was an ingrained departmental practice. Had these Commanders been terminated, they would have sued for reinstatement. The subsequent court proceedings would have revealed the practice and the City of Philadelphia and its Police Department would have had a clouded reputation that would have lasted for years. In addition, there was a financial incentive to put this scandal to rest. The Republican Convention was slated to take place in Philadelphia in the year 2000. An ongoing scandal such as this would damage Philadelphia's reputation as one of the safest large cities in the country and jeopardize hundreds of millions of dollars in revenue projected from conventioneers and tourists. In addition, Mayor Rendell had his political eye on becoming Governor of Pennsylvania. The last thing he needed was placing himself at the center of a scandal involving his Police Department.

During my interview for Dateline NBC, I detailed the process the Police Department used to downgrade certain crimes. The totality of the interview did not appear on television. One of the things I told them was how the department hid reported rapes in which there was not an apprehended suspect. If a rape victim's description of a rapist was not specific; if the rape victim was intoxicated; or if the rape victim was suspected of being a prostitute, the crime would be downgraded to an "investigation of person". This action would end the investigation. A rapist was free to victimize another person. I think the team that interviewed me found this practice a little too bizarre to televise. After all, what civilized Police Department would underreport this serious violation of the human body?

I remembered responding to a disturbance call in Southwest Philadelphia's 12th Police District. There were three children at home with their father. There was a boy of about nine years of age, a girl of about ten years of age, and another girl of thirteen years of age. The mother was at work this particular Friday evening. The father called the thirteen year old girl upstairs to the second floor while the two younger children remained in the first floor living room. Once the thirteen year old girl arrived at the top of the stairs, the father pulled her into a bedroom. He began to fondle her between her legs and attempted to remove her underwear. She fought off his advances. There was a violent struggle which resulted in the girl falling down a flight of stairs to the first floor. The father (this is her blood father) came down the stairs and began to kick her. This was when the older sister ran to a telephone and called the Police Department by dialing "911". Several male Police Officers arrived during this first call. The thirteen year old girl was frozen in terror. She would not talk to the Police Officers. The father told them that there was only a small discipline problem that he was trying to resolve. The Police Officers left.

The father began another attack on the teenager. Another call was made to the Police Department. This time I responded along with a female Police Officer. The thirteen year old girl was still terrified. The father maintained that there was no problem. One of the younger children told a Police Officer that the father had thrown his sister down the stairs and had kicked her. This was not discipline. The female Police Officer took the thirteen year old girl into the kitchen and away from the throng of Police Officers and her father. There, the thirteen year old revealed what had occurred in the second floor bedroom. She, also, revealed that on several occasions, the father would take her to his mother's home. He would take her to a bedroom and fondle her. There was no intercourse, just the most intimate of fondling. Once this was revealed, we arrested the father.

As was established practice, the thirteen year old was transported to the Children's Hospital of Philadelphia for examination. I went there because I was the arresting Officer and I was charged with completing the report. That required me to go to the hospital, obtain a Physician's name and to wait for the arrival of Investigators from the Sex Crimes Unit. I arrived at about 11:30pm. My work shift was almost over, but I was not concerned about the lateness of the hour. I wanted to complete the assignment and to see a perverted father go to jail.

At approximately 12:15am, a male Police Officer and a female Police Officer from the Sex Crimes Unit arrived. The female Police Officer was an African-American Police Officer whom I knew because of her membership in the Guardian Civic League. She came into the hospital looking angry and impatient. I thought that it was because this unit's shift normally ended at 1:00am. Still, this was a crime. It was part of our job to pursue the investigation. She looked at my written report. She pulled off the yellow carbon copy of the report. Then she said words that shook me to my core. "This girl is lying. Nothing happened. Let me talk to her. I'll get the truth out of her." I directed this team to the room where the teenager was being tended to by the medical staff.

I could not believe that a person who was supposedly concerned about the welfare of disadvantaged people in the African-American community could have such a callous attitude about the attempted rape of a defenseless thirteen year old girl. Remember, that it took compassion and understanding for the young girl to reveal to the female Police Officer about the action of her father. Her brother and sister witnessed the pummeling their sister received although they did not have any knowledge about the attempted rape. I left the Sex Crimes team at the hospital. I had a very uneasy feeling about what would occur if they confronted this child in the aggressive manner they were evidencing to me.

The next day, my suspicions were confirmed. First, I looked at the arrest book. The father's name did not appear in it. Next, I looked at the "Part One Sheet". This offense should have appeared on it. It was not there. My report was re-written and re-coded as a "Minor Disturbance" no further action required. I protested loudly to the Operations Team and to my Sergeant. Both told me that the decision was left up to the Sex Crimes Unit as to whether or not further action was required. There was no doubt in my mind that the Sex Crimes Investigators intimidated the child into silence. That was an easy task to accomplish. No crime. No arrest. This child was victimized by the father and the Police Department. I had personal empirical evidence of this practice of downgrading rapes and attempted rapes, even when those crimes were committed against children. This was an abomination.

My focusing on rapes is important. According to local news media, between 1997 and 1999 there were six rapes in Center City Philadelphia that, retrospectively, appeared to have been committed by the same person. One rape of a twenty-three year old graduate student ended with her death. In 2001, there were a series of rapes which occurred in Fort Collins, Colorado. An unsigned letter sent to the Fort Collins Police Department about the sexual assaults there launched an investigation which linked a total of fourteen sexual assaults (six in Philadelphia and eight in Fort Collins) to Troy Graves. He was a former Center City resident who enlisted in the Air Force and was now stationed at an Air Force Base near Fort Collins. A Philadelphia Inquirer news article by Inquirer Staff Writers, Thomas Ginsberg, Larry Fish, and Thomas J. Gibbons, Jr. stated, "His attacks here also exposed deep problems in how Philadelphia investigated sexual assaults. Police repeatedly botched their investigations into the cases, labeling his first victim a liar, refusing to accept his second as an (sic) sexual-assault victim, and failing for months to make crucial DNA links." This was exactly the ineptitude and callousness I had outlined to Dateline NBC in the portion of their interview that was not televised.

By this time, I felt a great deal of accomplishment. I felt that I was an integral part of the Philadelphia Police Department's changing of an antiquated and dishonest crime reporting system. Indirectly, my interview on Dateline NBC may have be the fulcrum that leveraged the arrest of a murderer and serial rapist. As with the breaking up of the burglary ring in the 5th Police District, there would be no corporate pat on the back for my actions. It was not needed. My arms were long enough to accomplish that myself. I, always wanted to work for positive changes within the Police Department. Sometimes those actions came about because of my work the Guardian Civic League. At other times, I had to walk alone. As mentioned earlier, a Police Officer will have a paucity of allies when he/she takes a stand against corrupt and illegal activities by other Police Officers.

You would think that after the airing of my interview on Dateline NBC the harassment from Myrna and the ignorance of the Police Department would end. It did not. In July of 1999, I celebrated my birthday with cousins who lived in Wilmington, North Carolina. I had been doing this for years. This year, on my return home, my cousin David met me soon after my arrival at home. He was selling tickets to a family reunion that would be held soon in New Jersey. Not more than fifteen minutes after his arrival, someone rang my door bell. Two African-American Police Officers were standing there. They asked to enter. This was embarrassing. It was about 6:30pm.

They were at my home to serve me with a Protection Order taken out by Myrna. Myrna alleged that she had seen me sitting in a car outside of her residence on June 30, 1999. I showed the Police Officer my air flight tickets. These tickets showed that I boarded a flight out of Philadelphia early in the morning on June 30th and returned on July 6th. The allegation was absurd. The Police Officer was friendly. He stated that his hands were tied. He had to serve me with the petition and to give me a subpoena for a court appearance on August 2, 1999.

I had been through this before with this disturbed female. I thought the madness was over. It was not. I will condense this story by stating that we appeared before Judge Ida Chen in Domestic Relations Court (July

Term 1999, Number 7004). The Judge found that Myrna's allegation was unsubstantiated. Myrna fabricated this Protection Order only because of letters I had sent to the Mayor, to the Police Commissioner, and to the Internal Affairs Bureau. One or all of these entities decided it would be a good idea to send her copies of these letters. Her response was to file an abuse complaint against me. This was how the Police Department retaliated. This was their way of punishing me. They used a neurotic and vindictive female Police Officer in an attempt to first silence me. Secondly, certain members of the Police Department wanted to punish me for uncovering scandalous behavior in the 5th Police District and to punish me for participating in the revelation of improper crime reporting.

The Judge did characterize me as being "obsessive" in my quest to clear my name and in how I voiced my indignation to every relevant Philadelphia government official. My belief has always been that one comes into this world as an innocent. You live your life and when the light of the world has turned to darkness you leave a legacy. I have always valued my integrity. I was not going to leave a legacy of disgrace based on the maliciousness of a callous and vindictive Police Department. Other than my children, my integrity is the most precious thing I possess. As I have told every police and government official, I would fight to clear my name as long as I breathed.

It was anathema for me to leave at rest the malicious deceit used as a weapon by the Philadelphia Police Department to damage my name. They doubted my resolve. If the "feelings" of some were hurt, that was not my concern. When you set a fire, there is always the possibility that you will be burned by your own actions. I had completed a public service. Perhaps, some of the deceitful behavior of the Philadelphia Police Department that adversely affected every city citizen would end. Perhaps, lives would be saved and some properties not invaded. Perhaps, there would be a true reduction in crime not because of erasures but because of good leadership decisions. Optimism remained the ointment for the wounds of ignorance.

The Decision of a Lifetime

It was at this time that I decided to leave Philadelphia. This had been my home for fifty-four years. The harassment was not going to stop. The Police Department was unforgiving. I was wary of going outside of my residence because I was in fear of being falsely arrested. Even when I confined myself to home, there was no guarantee that I would not be served again with a bogus protection order or possibly be falsely accused of some crime.

Once I decided to move, I kept my intention secret. I shared it with no one except my oldest daughter and son. I notified my two daughters in Philadelphia about a month before I was due to leave. I notified the utility companies to close my account about two weeks before I left. I waited until the day before my day of departure to turn in my cable television equipment. It was an emotional event. It was a lonely event. I had not worked in months. My car was repossessed. My finances were near zero. All of this because of the actions of a scorned and distraught woman who allowed herself to be used by the Police Department.

On December 30, 1999 at about 4:30am, I walked out of my home carrying all that I could in a clothing bag, a large plastic container, and a suitcase. I left Philadelphia not knowing what fortunes or misfortunes I would face at my new destination in Georgia. Thanks to my son, Norman and my daughter, Monique I was able to navigate my first few tough months.

In a letter dated June 19, 2000, a Philadelphia lawyer representing Myrna sent a letter to my former address in Philadelphia. The United States Postal Service forwarded the letter to my proper address. The letter began, "My client, Myrna, informs me that you have once again instituted a pattern of repeated harassment of her." The situation with Myrna had moved from troubling to bizarre. It seemed as though the harassment would never end. Here, I was hundreds of miles away, wrapped up in concerns about a friend with terminal cancer, and the harassment continued. I penned a three-paged retort with about eight pages of attachments. By certified mail, I sent copies to this Lawyer and to the Philadelphia Police Commissioner.

I told the Lawyer and the Police Commissioner that Myrna was guilty of "barratry". Barratry is a legal term for a person who misuses the power of the court to harass someone or some company. I encouraged the lawyer and the Police Department to seek counseling for Myrna. I sent them documents which proved that Myrna had committed perjury in both Protection from Abuse Orders and during her testimony in Family Court. I provided them with the docket number from our appearance in Family Court. My hope was that they, just as I had done, would spend about $100.00 to obtain a copy of Judge Chen's opinion. After this letter there were no further complaints from this woman scorned. Likely, both the lawyer and the Police Department realized they were being used by a vindictive prevaricator who had brought and was going to bring problems to their doorstep.

I soon found that my involvement with the Philadelphia Police Department was not quite over. In May 2001, I contributed to an investigative report by the Philadelphia Daily News News entitled "Battered Cargo". It was an investigative report on injuries suffered by prisoners transported in Emergency Patrol Wagons by Philadelphia Police Officers. As a result of that report, the Philadelphia Police Department instituted new safety measures to lessen the likelihood of prisoners suffering injury while being transported by Police Officers. This was another instance in which lives may have been saved.

During the same period of time, State Senator Harold James, who was a former President of the Guardian Civic League, invited me to testify before the Pennsylvania Legislative Black Caucus's hearing concerning the "Police Department's Discriminatory Practices and Policies in the Commonwealth." I paid for my plane ticket and hotel stay because this was important to me. My quest to be a cog in the wheel of progressive change continued.

Integrity Control

There are some steps that the Philadelphia Police Department could have taken to either eliminate or reduce the incidence of protracted complicity and corruption in any Police Division. Depending on their construction, other municipal police departments may adapt these suggestions to fit their needs.

1. Each Police District Commander must be required to have a monthly community meeting.
   a. A discussion of monthly and yearly crime statistics should take place at each of these meetings.
   b. A Captain or above from the Internal Affairs Bureau must attend each Community Meeting. This Captain would be responsible for making a report to his superior and to the Police Commissioner about integrity concerns from the community during this meeting.
   c. Neither a District Commander nor a Divisional Commander should remain in that same assignment for more than three years.
2. Non-uniformed Police Officers working in undercover assignments.
   a. Police Officers in this status should be limited to a maximum of two years working in this status.
      (1) Police Officers in undercover status become much too familiar with the unsavory portion of our society. Officers in this status begin to take on the appearance and the mentality of the people they are investigating. In time, they will become

complacent and overly selective about whom they should target for arrest.

(2) My experience had shown that most corrupt undercover Police Officers are those who have spent an inordinate amount of time in that capacity. I once worked with an individual who had spent over ten years in as an undercover operative. He was an expert, who became adept at circumventing legal and departmental guidelines that adversely affected innocent people. He became known as a "farmer". A "farmer" is an officer who insures every Search Warrant has a fruitful end because he is skilled at "planting" evidence.

(3) Police Officers should spend no more than five years in any Police District. A fresh start every five years should be a morale booster. Certain business and community representatives might not be pleased with this directive. The Police Department and community representatives must realize that all Police Officers must demonstrate a sincere responsiveness to the needs of the communities in which they work. Some Police Officers are better communicators and they easily endear themselves to the community. It is the responsibility of the Police Department to insure that the greater majority of their officers are good communicators. Poor communication causes many avoidable problems. If a Police Officer cannot speak three sentences without resorting to profanity or culturally bigoted statements, then that Police Officer is a liability. The department must rid itself of liabilities.

(4) Each Police Officer must attend an annual Human Relations Seminar conducted by a local college or university. This seminar would be mandatory

every two years. A Police Commander must be present at each seminar. This Commander would be responsible for monitoring attentiveness and responsiveness to the material discussed. This seminar should take no more than one day. The Police Commissioner or his designee should insure that the content of this seminar is in compliance with departmental and legal policies.

(5) The Police Commissioner should establish a "hotline" available to Police Officers who want to report incidences of corrupt or complicit behavior among their co-workers. Each complaint must be investigated by an Internal Affairs Supervisor with a rank of Lieutenant or above. If a certain pattern of complaints are determined, the Police Commissioner must establish a thirty-day deadline for establishing the validity of the complaint. All complaints must be numbered and available to the public by written requests.

Epilog

In looking back over my recent years, I found that leaving behind the systemic and ingrained malfeasance of the Philadelphia Police Department and moving to Georgia rejuvenated my life. I was the caregiver for a close friend for a significant portion of my first year in Georgia. After her death, I secured a job with Crestline Hotels and Resorts because I needed to be around people. I needed to regain my trust in people. I sought only a part-time job as a Loss Prevention Officer. I was hired to a full-time position. Within two years, I was promoted to Security Director at the Georgia Tech Hotel and Conference Center. Eventually, I would be promoted to two other Management positions in disciplines not related to security. This was the emotional balm I needed to heal the wounds inflicted by the Philadelphia Police Department's Internal Affairs Bureau and Officer Myrna. I worked in this second career for thirteen years. I would never had been afforded this degree of success had I remained in Philadelphia.

I would like to believe that I worked for one of best Police Department's in the country. Because I have worked for only one, I can only make a judgement based on my experiences. Philadelphia's Police Department, like many, was ultra-conservative when it came to effecting positive changes that would benefit the community it served. It should never have taken hundreds of thousands of dollars in litigation fees that were paid for by Philadelphia's taxpayers for the department to realize that it did not reflect the racial demographic of its citizens. It should never have taken several years and several hundreds of thousands of dollars of taxpayer money before the department stopped fighting a progressive effort to put female Police Officers on equal footing as their male counterparts. In both of these occurrences, the Fraternal Order of Police Lodge #5 stood lock-step with the Police Department in a repressive stance against giving all citizens, regardless of their race or gender an equal opportunity to pursue a career in this noble profession.

I would have liked the Internal Affairs Bureau to have been more honest and more efficient in removing from the department those Officers who became criminals hiding behind a badge. It should never have been necessary for me to use surreptitious means to consummate the arrest of the leader of a burglary ring. The burglary ring leader used Police Officers as an integral part of his criminal enterprise. Ironically, some of the Police Officers I have alleged to have been involved with this criminal enterprise were neither fired nor disciplined. They were only transferred. That was the Philadelphia Police Department's way of finding guilt but not administering a penalty. In fact one member of that infamous 5 Squad ended his career in the Internal Affairs Bureau. That was how the Police Department rewarded bad cops who kept their mouths shut. Remember, this was consistent with the treatment received by the Organized Crime Instructor at the Police Academy. If you kept your mouth shut and ignored departmentally sanctioned injustices, you were an asset to the Philadelphia Police Department.

I have always revered my chosen profession as a Police Officer. Despite all of the turmoil this profession gave to me during my career and after my retirement, I still revere it. Being a Police Officer is an occupation with a built in opportunity to be a guardian of one's community. Unfortunately, as with bad teachers, bad doctors, and bad politicians it is a difficult and almost impossible job to dispose of the bad apples. The short cutters, those handicapped by a severe lack of integrity, and those who hide their heads in the sand while wrongdoing goes on around them keep a black cloud over the men and women of law enforcement.

Unless the informed public demands it, corruption will continue to flourish in Police Departments in Philadelphia and throughout the country. My career was in no way unique. There were others around me who saw what I saw but they refused to do what I did. From that woman who was transported in the trunk of a police car to the retaliatory burglary of a night club to the ignorance I faced with Internal Affairs Bureau compliant 97-XX8, there were Police Officers who observed or knew about what was occurring. They – did - nothing. They refused to submit even an anonymous report to the Police Department, to the news media, or to the Federal Government. I was foolish enough that I never submitted a report anonymously. Every Police Officer swears to uphold the constitutional laws of their country, their state, and their community. This is an almost sacred trust lain upon the shoulders of every Police Officer. Once you break that trust, you are a Police Officer in name only. Once you break that trust, you become a criminal of the lowest order.

Unfortunately, we live in a time when people who have no idea of what it takes to be a Police Officer and the dangers they face are taking cheap shots at every action taken by a Police Officer. I am not a part of that uninformed madness. Even bad Police Officers or Police Officers who make errors in judgement are entitled to a fair hearing to determine the propriety and legality of their actions. Every Police Officer is not a bad person. Most come to work and strive to protect you and to serve you. The public must learn to look at individuals and not paint all officers with the same broad brush. This is why I have tried to be as specific as possible about the persons whom I knew violated procedures and laws. They and they alone deserve the condemnation.

Staying politically informed and politically active may make impositions on your time, but it is the best way to assure you have a stable and committed Police Department. If the citizens of the Manayunk, Wissahickon, Andorra, and Roxborough sections of Philadelphia had shouted their outrage about the actions of certain Police Officers and Rocco Barba, that despicable incursion into their lives would have ended sooner. This is not my attempt to blame the victims. What happened in those communities was some people felt that their only option was to live within the constraints of the status quo. They felt their only option was to accept the alliance between a criminal and criminalized Police Officers.

The "no snitch" philosophy only guarantees that bad things will not only continue, but also they will get worse. That situation becomes exacerbated when those bad things are committed with the knowledge of and efforts of Police Officers.

I know there are thousands of good and committed Police Professionals going about the daily business of protecting their communities. My hope is that you have the courage to fight crime both outside and inside of your departments. From the dawn of the twentieth century when Lincoln Steffens described Philadelphia as "corrupt and contented" through the days when drug dealers took over neighborhoods, you will find that one of the first steps in setting up and maintaining a criminal enterprise is to seek out Police Officers who are easily corrupted. There is no way a band of criminals can take over a community without corrupt and complicit Police Officers. This fact is true whether you are talking about "The Bloods", "The Blackstone Rangers", or the "Mafia (aka Cosa Nostra)". At one point during the 1980's, an African-American based criminal organization had an operative within the Philadelphia Police Department. His job was to arrest competitors who were involved in narcotics trafficking.

Therefore, Police Officers are an ideal bellwether for the health of a community. In order to regain its health a community might have to suffer through the unpleasantries of virtual diarrhea and reverse peristalsis to rid itself of the virus called apathy. Apathy leads directly to corruption and complicity in government. Corruption and complicity lead to the denial of certain liberties guaranteed by this country's Declaration of Independence.

This most precious of documents states, ".....all men are created equal and endowed by their Creator with certain unalienable rights, that these are the rights to life, liberty and the pursuit of Happiness." You cannot enjoy these rights without a competent and committed Police Department. A complete cleansing itself of corrupt and complicit behavior is the only way for a community to regain its health. Criminals, whether or not they wear uniforms need to be either removed from society or restricted in how they impact their communities. That removal involves imprisonment or a highly restrictive monitoring by penal authorities via our court systems.

If Police Officers remain consistent throughout their careers by doing their job with unfettered integrity, their communities and their country will stand behind them. Police Officers cannot always look for a pat on the back from their superiors or communities for a job well done. Sometimes the inner satisfaction of knowing that you have done your honest best to serve your country, your community, and your family will be all that you receive and most times that should be enough. There will always be Police Officers who have tendencies that lean them toward criminality.

Local, state, and federal governments should have zero tolerance for these weak-willed integrity challenged public servants. Only then will we all be free to live our lives with confidence in the integrity of our Police Departments. We should never accept less than that from our government, police departments, and ourselves.

The End

Printed in the United States
By Bookmasters